THE RISE OF CITIES

TimeFrame

Other Publications:
THE AMERICAN INDIANS
THE ART OF WOODWORKING
LOST CIVILIZATIONS
ECHOES OF GLORY
THE NEW FACE OF WAR
HOW THINGS WORK
WINGS OF WAR
CREATIVE EVERYDAY COOKING
COLLECTOR'S LIBRARY OF THE UNKNOWN
CLASSICS OF WORLD WAR II
TIME-LIFE LIBRARY OF CURIOUS AND UNUSUAL FACTS
AMERICAN COUNTRY
VOYAGE THROUGH THE UNIVERSE
THE THIRD REICH
THE TIME-LIFE GARDENER'S GUIDE
MYSTERIES OF THE UNKNOWN
FIX IT YOURSELF
FITNESS, HEALTH & NUTRITION
SUCCESSFUL PARENTING
HEALTHY HOME COOKING
UNDERSTANDING COMPUTERS
LIBRARY OF NATIONS
THE ENCHANTED WORLD
THE KODAK LIBRARY OF CREATIVE PHOTOGRAPHY
GREAT MEALS IN MINUTES
THE CIVIL WAR
PLANET EARTH
COLLECTOR'S LIBRARY OF THE CIVIL WAR
THE EPIC OF FLIGHT
THE GOOD COOK
WORLD WAR II
HOME REPAIR AND IMPROVEMENT
THE OLD WEST

For information on and a full description of
any of the Time-Life Books series listed above,
please call 1-800-621-7026 or write:
Reader Information
Time-Life Customer Service
P.O. Box C-32068
Richmond, Virginia 23261-2068

This volume is one in a series that tells the story
of humankind. Other books in the series include:

THE RISE OF CITIES

TimeFrame

BY THE EDITORS OF TIME-LIFE BOOKS

TIME-LIFE BOOKS, ALEXANDRIA, VIRGINIA

Time-Life Books is a division
of Time Life Inc.,
a wholly owned subsidiary of
THE TIME INC. BOOK COMPANY

TIME-LIFE BOOKS

PRESIDENT: Mary N. Davis

MANAGING EDITOR: Thomas H.
Flaherty
Director of Editorial Resources:
Elise D. Ritter-Clough
Executive Art Director: Ellen Robling
Director of Photography and Research:
John Conrad Weiser
Editorial Board: Dale M. Brown, Janet
Cave, Roberta Conlan, Laura Foreman,
Jim Hicks, Blaine Marshall, Rita Thievon
Mullin, Henry Woodhead
*Assistant Director of Editorial Resources /
Training Manager:* Norma E. Shaw

PUBLISHER: Robert H. Smith

Associate Publisher: Sandra Lafe Smith
Editorial Director: Russell B. Adams, Jr.
Marketing Director: Anne C. Everhart
Director of Production Services:
Robert N. Carr
Production Manager: Prudence G. Harris
Supervisor of Quality Control:
James King

EUROPEAN EDITOR: Ellen Phillips
Design Director: Ed Skyner
Director of Editorial Resources:
Samantha Hill
Chief Sub-Editor: Ilse Gray
Assistant Design Director: Mary Staples

Correspondents: Elisabeth Kraemer-Singh
(Bonn); Christine Hinze (London);
Christina Lieberman (New York); Maria
Vincenza Aloisi (Paris); Ann Natanson
(Rome). Valuable assistance was also
provided by: Barry Anthony, Jennifer Iker
(Alexandria, Virginia); Wibo van de Linde
(Amsterdam); Mirka Gondicas (Athens);
Brigid Grauman (Brussels); Martha de la
Cal (Lisbon); Elizabeth Brown (New
York); Josephine du Brusle (Paris); Ann
Wise (Rome); Dick Berry (Tokyo); Angela
Luker, Traudl Lessing (Vienna).

TIME FRAME
(published in Britain as
TIME-LIFE HISTORY OF THE WORLD)

SERIES EDITOR: Charles Boyle

Editorial Staff for *The Rise of Cities*
Editor: Fergus Fleming
Designer: Rachel Gibson
Researchers: Caroline Lucas (principal),
Sheila Corr
Sub-Editors: Frances Willard,
Luci Collings, Tim Cooke
Design Assistant: Sandra Archer
Editorial Assistant: Molly Sutherland

Picture Department
Picture Administrator: Amanda Hindley
Picture Coordinator: Zoë Spencer

Editorial Production
Production Assistant: Emma Veys
Editorial Department: Theresa John,
Debra Lelliott, Juliet Lloyd-Price

U.S. EDITION

Assistant Editor: Barbara Fairchild
Quarmby
Copy Coordinator: Ann Lee Bruen
Picture Coordinator: Barry Anthony

Editorial Operations
Production: Celia Beattie
Library: Louise D. Forstall
Computer Composition: Deborah G. Tait
(Manager), Monika D. Thayer, Janet Barnes
Syring, Lillian Daniels
Interactive Media Specialist: Patti H. Cass

Special Contributors: Neil Fairbairn, Robert
Irwin, Michael Kerrigan, Martin Leighton,
Alan Lothian, John Man (text); David E.
Manley (index).

CONSULTANTS

General:
PETER CLARK, Professor of Economic and
Social History, and Director of the Center for
Urban History, University of Leicester, Eng-
land

Early Cities:
TERENCE C. MITCHELL, Former Keeper of
Western Asiatic Antiquities, British Museum,
London

Classical Cities:
ANDREW WALLACE-HADRILL, Professor
of Classics, University of Reading, England

Asian Cities:
K. N. CHAUDHURI, Professor of the Economic History of Asia, School of Oriental
and African Studies, University of London

HUGH KENNEDY, Reader in Medieval
History, University of Saint Andrews, Fife,
Scotland

Medieval and Pre-Industrial Cities:
PETER CLARK, Professor of Economic and
Social History, and Director of the Center
for Urban History, University of Leicester,
England

Industrial and Modern Cities:
MARTIN DAUNTON, Professor of Modern History, University College, University
of London

Library of Congress Cataloging in
Publication Data

The Rise of cities / by the editors of Time-Life
Books.
    p.   cm.—(Time frame)
    Includes bibliographical references (p.   )
    and index.
    ISBN 0-8094-6487-X
    ISBN 0-8094-6488-8 (lib. bdg.)
    1. Cities and towns—History.
    I. Time-Life Books. II. Series.
HT111.R53 1991
909'.09732—dc20   90-25530
                                       CIP

CONTENTS

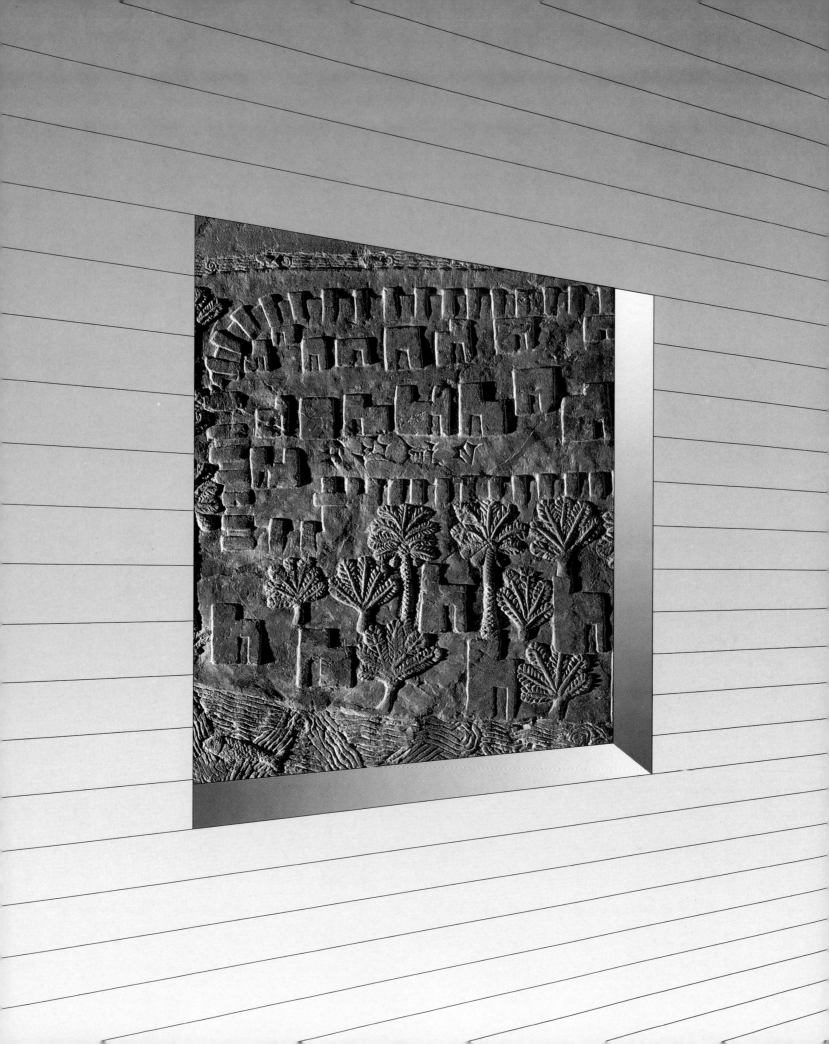

THE URBAN PIONEERS

1 Mud, the ubiquitous mud of the alluvial plains of southern Mesopotamia, was the material from which the world's first civilization was built. Mud, formed into uniform rectangular blocks, was used in the construction of houses, temples, and city walls. Mud, rolled flat into tablets, was the medium on which citizens recorded their commercial transactions, their laws, and their religious rituals. Mud, formed and fired, produced cooking and storage utensils. Mud, molded into human and animal figurines, represented the early sculptors' view of the world. But above all, mud provided the fertile topsoil that nourished the crops on which cities depended.

If the stands of wheat and barley failed, so did the city. And not just through lack of food. For crops meant more than mere sustenance: An agricultural surplus freed farmers from the field, allowing them to become artisans or traders; the organization of essential irrigation projects provided a hierarchy of rulers and administrators; the export of grain paid for the import of luxury goods; and the subsequent rise in wealth attracted immigrants and merchants from the surrounding countryside. Jobs, government, things to buy, and people to meet—the hallmarks of any modern city—all, ultimately, depended on mud.

The Middle Eastern civilization of Sumer first rose from the mud of Mesopotamia in about 3500 BC, alongside the life-giving waters of the Tigris and Euphrates rivers. The Sumerian cities were by no means the first in the world: As early as 8000 BC, some 3,000 people had dwelled within the walls of Jericho, a city situated by a gushing freshwater spring in the lower Jordan Valley. But the Sumerians' achievement was to coalesce a number of such isolated settlements into a coherent whole, bound by the same rulers, laws, gods, and culture. As pioneers of civilization the Sumerians were, for a while, unique on the face of the earth. But other civilizations were soon to follow. The mud of Egypt, of China, and of India was just as productive as that of Mesopotamia, and along the banks of some of the world's mightiest rivers—the Nile, the Yellow, and the Indus—small riparian communities were independently blossoming into full-fledged civilizations.

Once lighted, the fuse was impossible to extinguish. Civic populations grew steadily as a percentage of the global total, occasionally clustering in spectacular star bursts of achievement: In the first century BC, Rome was the world's first city of one million people; Changan (Xi'an), capital of imperial China, reached the same mark just a few hundred years later. Outstanding wonders of their time, they and other, similar cities were just a presage of things to come. For with the dawn of the industrial age, humanity's sputtering progress toward the city turned into an explosion of urbanization. Asphalt was slapped down, walls were thrown up, and cities expanded over the surrounding countryside in a flurry of bricks, mortar, and concrete. By 1990, with metropolises containing up to 20 million inhabitants—where, indeed, it was possible

Date palms and a river teeming with fish grace the city of Madaktu, in present-day Iran, in a relief of the seventh century BC. Belying this scene of rural tranquillity, however, most of the city's houses are tightly packed within the confines of a defensive wall. In a world subject to the threat of both human and animal predators, sturdy defenses were a prerequisite for urban existence, creating a clear boundary between the civilized community within and the dangerous zone without. But any security the citizens of Madaktu felt was illusory: This scene was carved by their warlike neighbors, the Assyrians, soon after they had overrun the city.

7

Ohne of the wealthiest trade centers in Mesopotamia—and by about 2000 BC, center of the flourishing Sumerian civilization—the city of Ur stood as a paradigm of early urban life. Its crowded domestic dwellings, bazaars, and tiny alleys clustered around the huge, sprawling temple complex, which contained the stepped ziggurat dedicated to the moon-god Nanna. The city, raised high above the surrounding flood plain through successive building on top of crumbled mud-brick structures, was protected by a wall a mile and a quarter long and a pair of broad, encircling canals linked to the nearby Euphrates River. The canals not only allowed maritime trade access to Ur's two inner-city harbors but also fed the extensive irrigation system that crisscrossed the surrounding plain.

Like most cities of the age, Ur's existence was defined by the endeavors of its farmers. The fertile land supplied an abundance of cereal crops, beans, and vegetables, as well as providing pasturage for the flocks of sheep whose fleece supplied the city's thriving textile trade. At the same time, this agricultural plenty had freed a large portion of the population to concentrate on other tasks. Weaving, metalworking, and stone carving were just a few of the skilled occupations open to the some 30,000 citizens who dwelled in the city.

A terra-cotta model of an oxcart from the Indian center of Mohenjo-Daro carries the vital grain that sustained all early cities.

to pick out individual centers amid the vast conurbations that covered some regions—people no longer needed to come to the town: The town was coming to them.

But it was not the size of cities that mattered so much as the changes they wrought in the lives of their inhabitants. Their teeming confines acted as seedbeds for social change, the exigencies of cheek-by-jowl coexistence spurring humanity to formulate new codes of behavior. The very concept of law, for example, differentiated the earliest urban dwellers from their rural cousins; the demands of the demos, or ordinary people of classical Athens, produced democracy; and the experience of nineteenth-century industrial cities prompted Karl Marx and Friedrich Engels to write the *Communist Manifesto*. Nor was the change limited to politics. In art and architecture, education and entertainment, crime and commerce, indeed in almost every field of endeavor, the close human interaction of the city brought innovation.

From mud to metropolis, the rise of cities has been one of the most momentous phenomena in the history of humankind—and indeed of the planet. For some four and one-half billion years, life on earth had evolved according to the laws of natural selection. Each plant and animal existed within its own ecological niche, adapted to perform a given task within a given habitat, in an interdependent chain of survival. Humans, no less than any other life form, were restricted by this pattern. They may have been more intelligent than most creatures, but their role was still limited to that of the hunter-gatherer, roaming the inhabitable areas of the globe in search of food.

With the advent of cities, however, the mold was shattered irrevocably. By transforming their habitat, humans had found a new niche in which to survive—indeed, not just one niche, but as many as the mind could conceive. For the key to city life was opportunity. Freed from the constraints of a hand-to-mouth existence, city dwellers could turn their skills to a plethora of specialized trades: basketry, potmaking, spinning, weaving, leatherworking, carpentry, and stoneworking—whatever the market would bear. And as the market became larger and more diverse, so did the number of opportunities. The impact of this seemingly simple move was enormous. No longer did people need to battle to survive as hunters or gatherers, adapting over the centuries to become ever more proficient at these tasks; there was now an almost unlimited range of occupations open to them. Effectively, humanity had jumped several rungs up the evolutionary ladder.

It was not a sudden leap, more a series of infinitesimal shuffles that took place over thousands of years. And paradoxically, it was nature itself that gave impetus to this move away from the natural order. For as the last Ice Age waned, about 10,000 BC, the earth came to life again. As the glaciers melted, continents that had previously groaned under sheets of ice were revealed to the air. And the water that had been locked in frigid immobility was released into the atmosphere. Sea levels rose, and rain-bearing winds began to circle the globe, bringing fertility to previously barren areas. In this bountiful world, it became less and less necessary for humans to wander in search of food. In some areas, it was possible to set up year-round encampments where a community's needs could be supplied entirely from the surrounding countryside. From settlement to exploitation of the land was a short step. By about 7000 BC, these early villagers had mastered the art of domesticating crops and animals, and they had moved from being sedentary nomads to full-fledged farmers.

The new way of life was astonishingly productive—the same area of land that could support one hunter-gatherer now fed some 200 farmers—and population rose accordingly. Laborers who were not required in the fields were free to engage in specialized crafts. Walls sprang up around these farming settlements to safeguard both the inhabitants and their carefully hoarded stores of grain from marauding nomads. The allure of security—combined with plenty of food and the availability of basic manufactured products—acted as a magnet to other farmers in the neighborhood, and village populations grew apace.

Not everybody who came to these communities came to stay. Many were transient merchants. Since farmers had first begun to hoard their surplus crops, they had realized that their grain could do more than just feed their own people. It could also be bartered for necessities or even luxuries that were available only in other regions. Gradually, the contacts of traders spread farther and farther afield, exporting new technologies such as metalworking and glassmaking, and bringing home not only new goods but new ideas.

A necessary tool of commercial transactions was the ability to record the nature of goods and their amount. From the fourth millennium BC, entrepreneurs in the Middle East were recording their business deals with clay tokens imprinted with symbolic outlines that were universally understood—for instance, a horizontal crescent might represent horned cattle. And in time these symbols developed into a pictographic script that could record not only objects but also verbs. The pictograph for "eat," for example, would show an image of a head juxtaposed with an outline that could be understood to mean "food."

These advances had a profound effect on the social structure of the farming communities. The old, simple loyalties to family or clan enlarged as people banded together on mutually beneficial projects, such as irrigation or defense of their lands. As jobs became more specialized and artisans congregated to serve the needs of the neighborhood, workaday agricultural villages became small market towns where, say, a farmer could buy a bronze plow, a pottery storage jar, or a wooden bed in exchange for his surplus crops or livestock. Social stratification began to emerge as successful farmers bought land from their less-fortunate fellows, who were perforce reduced to earning a living by selling their labor. A mercantile class created a requirement for laws—codified by a newly literate population of scribes—on a host of matters such as commercial transactions, shipment fees, fair wages, the regulation of prices, and exchange rates for precious metals such as silver and gold. And as the number of regulations swelled, central governments and civil services arose to administer the town's multifarious activities. And when these interdependent factors coalesced in a single society, a city was created. In about 3500 BC, it fell to the Sumerians in southern Mesopotamia to lead the world into civilization.

A major beneficiary of the glaciers' great thaw was the Fertile Crescent, a verdant arc of territory circumscribed by the Persian Gulf, the course of the Tigris and Euphrates rivers into the mountains of Anatolia, and the eastern shoreline of the Mediterranean. It was good ground, its plains home to extensive stands of wheat and barley, and its lightly forested hillsides teeming with wildlife. This bounty was too great for the region's hunter-gatherers to ignore, and they gradually began to abandon their nomadic lifestyles and settle down in farming communities.

Among those to do so were the Sumerians, whose origins possibly lay to the northeast of the Fertile Crescent but who had, by the fourth millennium BC, found their way to the lush grassland surrounding the lower stretches of the Tigris and

Euphrates, just above the point where the two rivers converged in their southward flow to the Persian Gulf.

It was an unlikely spot for the birth of civilization. There was neither stone nor timber for building; there were no gems or precious metals for export—there was little, in fact, besides acres and acres of mud. But that was enough. Centuries of flooding by the Tigris and Euphrates had sloughed off a rich layer of alluvial sediment over the surrounding plains, and it was a relatively simple matter to divert the river water into irrigation channels that turned an arid expanse into an agricultural gold mine. The seemingly endless productivity of the land was enhanced still further by the Sumerians' development of a sturdy, bronze-bladed plow, and by about 3000 BC, their invention of the wheel. The waters that nourished the land also provided a convenient trade route along which excess grain could be exported in exchange for commodities the region lacked.

Harvests came and went, food stocks grew, and farming populations swelled. Villages became towns, which in turn developed into cities. By the middle of the third millennium BC, the Sumerians had established a political and cultural hegemony over much of Mesopotamia. In a dozen or so of its communities, Sumer had taken a lead in the improvement of irrigation, the development of trade, the formation of legal codes, and the establishment of central governments. And from these grew city-states—Ur, Eridu, Uruk, Nippur, and Larsa being among the first—whose authority encompassed both the city and the surrounding farmland.

Of all the cultural ties that bound these city-states, that of religion left the deepest imprint on the urban landscape. Each city had adopted a god or, according to Sumerian mythology, had been chosen by a god for an earthly abode. The city was believed to be the personal property of the deity and his or her family, and as a result, the temple, raised on a platform of mud, was the focal point of civic life. When a temple fell down, a new one was built on the holy site, and as successive buildings rose on ever-higher terraces of debris, the temple took on the form of a stepped structure—known as a ziggurat—towering above the maze of surrounding dwellings.

The city god communicated with citizens through a human representative known as the *en,* while secular decisions, in the early cities at least, were arrived at democratically through a bicameral system consisting of an assembly of all free citizens and an upper house of "elders." In times of emergency, however, the citizens would appoint a *lugal,* or king. On occasion, the offices of lugal and en were combined, making the king the god's earthly representative. Over time, the office of lugal became permanent and, finally, hereditary, giving rise to dynastic power. At the same time, as wealthier families bought up fields and hired landless peasants to farm them, they became the nucleus of a nobility.

A silver model captures the sweeping lines of the boats that plied Mesopotamia's waterways during the third millennium BC. Constructed from tightly packed reed bundles lashed together and coated with waterproofing bitumen, such flat-bottomed vessels were invaluable for navigating the region's shallow lakes and marshes. Long before overland routes came into general use, river transportation was the primary link between urban trading centers in the ancient world.

The distinctive silhouette of the ziggurat would have been a familiar sight to any Sumerian citizen traveling between the region's cities. Equally—and depressingly—familiar would have been the city walls. For, despite their strong cultural affinities, the city-states of Sumer remained individual and fiercely independent. Often built within sight of one another, and with their outlying fields merging, they were in constant dispute over irrigation rights and boundaries. This antagonism frequently erupted into armed conflict. And even when not fighting one another, the Sumerians kept a watchful eye out for raiding tribes, who regularly swept in from the desert to their west or the mountain ranges to the east. It was not until 2334 BC, some 1,000 years after the emergence of the first cities, that a king called Sargon of Akkad seized control,

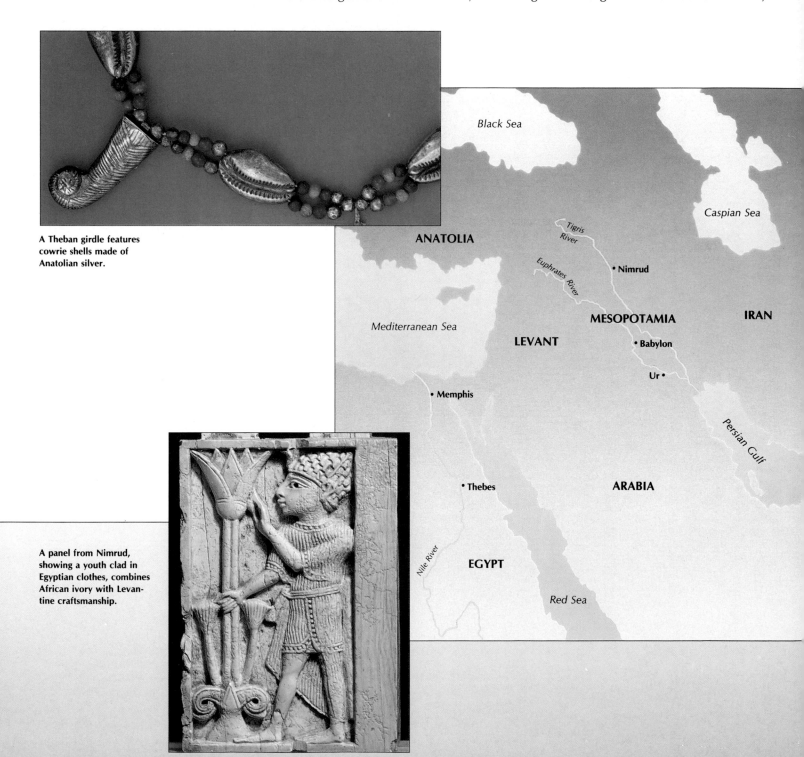

A Theban girdle features cowrie shells made of Anatolian silver.

A panel from Nimrud, showing a youth clad in Egyptian clothes, combines African ivory with Levantine craftsmanship.

first of Sumer, then of all Mesopotamia, and imposed a centralized system of government, based in one city, to run the whole country.

The inheritors of Sargon's unification of Mesopotamia were the kings of Ur, a city that in 2112 BC rose to a pinnacle of prosperity and governed the whole of Mesopotamia, from the Anatolian mountains to the Persian Gulf. During the following century, the rulers of this empire embarked upon a vigorous program of public building, which was supervised by specially trained architects. Ur's ziggurat was rebuilt in the form of a three-stage structure of beautiful proportions. Each terrace was cased by baked bricks decorated with buttresses and mosaics and possibly planted with trees. The whole, sixty-five feet high, was topped by a shrine, reached by a series

Afghan lapis lazuli adorns a head ornament made for a citizen of Ur.

Trade was the hallmark of the world's emergent cities. The surplus food produced from the surrounding countryside not only freed farmers to become artisans but provided a commodity that could be bartered for essentials, such as building materials, or as citizens grew wealthier, for luxury goods—gold, silver, ivory, and semiprecious stones. Nor was the trade confined to raw materials. Some cities prospered as manufacturing centers, using their new pools of skilled labor to turn crude imports into polished masterpieces for export.

As merchants ventured farther and farther afield, the tendrils of commerce reached out to link first cities and then, ultimately, civilizations. Into Mesopotamia, for example, flowed Egyptian gold, Lebanese timber, Anatolian obsidian, Indian carnelian, and lapis lazuli from the mountains of Afghanistan. By ship, donkey train, camel caravan, and oxcart, the world's resources were mobilized to serve the appetites of civilization.

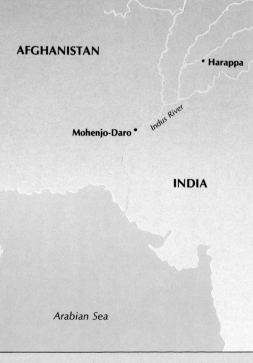

AFGHANISTAN

• Harappa

Indus River

Mohenjo-Daro •

INDIA

Arabian Sea

LINKS OF COMMERCE

of stairways, which was dedicated to Ur's patron deity, the moon-god Nanna. The precinct around the ziggurat was enclosed by walls and a religious complex of open courtyards and chapels. Outside this enclosure stood a royal palace, a temple storehouse, and a residence for the high priests. It was an architectural concept that was to be echoed in cities throughout Mesopotamia for another 1,500 years.

Around Ur's temple and royal complex lay the city proper—a 150-acre maze of two-story mud-brick dwellings arranged along winding streets and alleyways. There was little attempt at planned growth, and houses sprang up according to the accidents of landownership. The streets were unpaved and in times of heavy rainfall turned into a deep mire. The streets were not wide enough to accommodate wheeled vehicles, which were probably left at the city gates, all further movement within the walls being that of people or pack animals. To protect this fragile traffic from injury, the corners of the houses were rounded, and mounting blocks were provided in the streets for the convenience of riders.

A certain amount of respect was reserved for public rights: "If a wall is threatening to fall and the authorities have brought the fact to the knowledge of its owner," ran one admonitory law, "and if he does not strengthen the wall, which then collapses and causes a freeman's death, then it is a capital offense." But little attention was paid to public sanitation, although the temples themselves were fitted with impressive drains—perforated, baked-clay pipes that sank some forty feet into a potsherd-lined dry well. Defenses were not neglected—the whole city was protected by a massive, sloping rampart surrounded by a sturdy, baked-brick wall—but in the temporary peace granted by unification, citizens felt secure enough to live in suburbs, which stretched about a mile beyond the city walls. And beyond them lay the irrigated fields on whose produce Ur depended.

Among Ur's 20,000 citizens were priests, temple staff, scribes, administrators, schoolteachers, and every kind of artisan from riveters to carpenters. But perhaps the most valued members of the community were the merchants. Inside the city walls were two artificial harbors linked to the Euphrates by canals. And from here Ur's merchant marine set sail for the Persian Gulf and the city's major trading partner, the small island of Dilmun—modern-day Bahrain.

From this bustling entrepôt, they returned with luxury goods to suit the most sophisticated tastes—gold and silver vessels of the finest workmanship, jewels, intricate beaded headdresses, toilet boxes, and cosmetics. The seal stones of merchants, with which they marked imports and exports, and bills of lading written on clay tablets, detailed a far-flung web of commerce that stretched from the Indus Valley and Afghanistan in the east to Egypt and Lebanon in the west. One such tally from the early second millennium BC showed an incoming ship to have carried gold, copper ore, pearls, ivory, hardwoods, and precious stones.

With bureaucratic zeal, scribes recorded nearly every aspect of commerce and the administration of the state, using a wedge-shape stylus to write on tablets of flattened clay. The old pictographic script had developed into a rectilinear form for easier inscription, and by about 2500 BC, it was being used to represent spoken language, thus enabling the writer to express ideas and not simply record commodities. With this new tool of communication, scribes recorded the numbers of laborers working in the temple's fields, and the amount of work involved in cutting reeds, shearing livestock, or weaving bolts of cloth. Issues of beer and food rations, which was the way wages were paid, were listed; gifts of animals to state officials for "services

rendered" were recorded, as were sacrificial offerings to the gods and gifts to the king from foreign ambassadors and vassals.

Considerable attention was devoted to the administration of the king's wide dominions. Among the officials who worked in Ur's temple complex were the treasurer; ministers of war, agriculture, justice, and housing; the controller of the royal household; the master of the royal harem; and directors of livestock, dairy work, fishing, and donkey transport. Mesopotamia was divided into between forty and fifty city-states, each governed by an *ensi* who was usually directly answerable to the king. To prevent an ensi from building up too much local power, he was frequently transferred from district to district. The commanders of district garrisons were also directly answerable to the king, and if a dispute arose between a district commander and an ensi, it was resolved in a court of law. An efficient system of messengers was established to ensure that the king was regularly informed of events in outlying districts.

Ur's dominance of Mesopotamia was to last a scant century. But in the centuries to come, the system of sound central administration and social cohesion established by the Sumerians of Ur survived. Time and again, conquerors or invaders discovered there was no better system; so they adapted it to their purposes.

Only three centuries separated the beginning of Egyptian civilization from that of its neighbor Mesopotamia. Both civilizations sprang from the same conjunction of natural and social causes, but Egypt, inward-looking and deeply conservative, developed in a strikingly different way.

Like its Mesopotamian equivalent, the rich alluvial soil deposited annually with the flooding of the Nile was fertile ground. And by about 3500 BC, its surplus crops were nurturing a scattered civilization that had developed skilled crafts, a pantheon of gods, and the art of writing in hieroglyphs. But unlike Mesopotamia, Egypt was a closed country. Bounded on both sides by desert, the Nile Valley was relatively safe from outside invasion. And it was not long before one king achieved hegemony over the whole area, establishing the capital city of a united kingdom at Memphis, just south of the Nile Delta.

This ancient Egyptian kingdom, which anticipated the unification of Mesopotamia by some eight centuries, was based on a highly stratified society that consisted of a descending hierarchy of the gods, the king, the dead, and humanity. The pharaoh, or king, considered to be the earthly embodiment of a god, stood at a pinnacle of power, communicating with his subjects through his priests—often members of his own family—who were at the same time the administrators of the state. This powerful oligarchy, numbering about 5,000 in 3000 BC, ruled a population estimated at 870,000, most of whom were engaged in primitive agriculture.

The maintenance of power depended on the propagation of the cult of the god-king and the awe in which he was held. The early pharaohs traveled their dominions ceaselessly, impressing their subjects in grand style. At Memphis, for instance, the royal palace and administrative center consisted of a huge, rectangular pavilion made from wood and matting, and hung with bright carpets. It had elaborately carved timber pillars inlaid with gold, yet the whole could be easily dismantled to accompany the pharaoh on his royal progress.

The reverence accorded to the pharaohs had a direct impact on city life. Although cities would have originally been surrounded by a wall—Egyptian nomads were no less threatening to settled farmers than those of Mesopotamia—the unifying presence

THE HUB OF THE COMMUNITY

More than just religious centers, Mesopotamian temples played an integral part in urban life, using the revenues from their vast landholdings to support the communities around them. Their granaries and other reserves enabled them to feed the population when a harvest failed, ransom prisoners, float merchants in need of capital, or tide a poor farmer over to the next season—often without interest. They also provided shelter for the homeless, taking care of orphans, illegitimate offspring, and children given to the temple by poor families.

One such benefactor was the temple *(right)* dedicated to the goddess Ishtar-Kititum. Constructed around 2000 BC in the city of Neribtum (modern Ischali), it comprised three separate shrines and a series of administrative buildings grouped around a spacious courtyard. The whole complex, as befitted its central role in the community, was raised ten feet above ground level on a solidly built terrace faced with kiln-fired bricks set in bitumen. The main shrine, which also contained the temple treasury, stood at an even higher level than the rest. Massive grooved towers flanked each entrance, adding extra authority to a structure that already dominated the town and surrounding countryside.

An impression from a stone seal discovered in the archives of the temple of Ishtar-Kititum depicts a worshiper, accompanied by a goddess, approaching a bearded figure enthroned on a dais—possibly the city's ruler.

IN SERVICE TO THE GODS

Brightly painted wooden figures of 1900 BC solemnly bear victuals for their deceased master. Such figures were placed in Egyptian tombs to serve the dead during their journey through the afterlife.

Scribes, such as this assiduous pair depicted in an early-fourteenth-century BC Egyptian tomb relief, monitored the complicated religious and commercial transactions of the ancient world's great temples.

The flow of humanity through the temples of the ancient world was ceaseless. Not only were they places of individual worship, where citizens left votive offerings to secure blessings or avert evil, but their day-to-day functioning involved the use of every skill and profession practiced in the city.

In Mesopotamia, the soothing and appeasement of the gods demanded battalions of priests, singers, and musicians. These, in turn, required a sizable force of household staff—cooks, maids, and cleaners. No less important were the temple's secular operations: Regiments of slaves labored in the temple's fields and granaries, while armies of local artisans toiled to supply the holy precinct with necessities such as textiles, pottery vessels, and furniture. Indeed, some temples became vast trading estates, with areas for manufacturing—spinning, tanning, weaving, and milling—storage, and distribution. And, overseeing all, there was a senior corps of scribes and officials that administered the smooth running of operations, allocating labor and resources, drawing up land surveys, recording donations, totting up income, and listing expenditures.

In Egypt, too, temples were bustling centers that combined trade and administration with worship. Among their many workshops, there were even special schools where would-be bureaucrats could learn to read and write. Nor was all this activity solely for the benefit of the living. The Egyptian dead were expected to have much the same requirements as they did when alive, and temple precincts could encompass entire cities specially built for life beyond the grave.

A votive stele, or stone slab, dedicated in 1200 BC to the Egyptian god Ptah, bears a multitude of ears to ensure the supplicant's prayer is heard.

An alabaster effigy of a worshiper from the goddess Nintu's sanctuary in the Mesopotamian city of Khafajah intercedes for a citizen in 2600 BC.

Carved in green serpentine and white limestone, a model of a female worshiper sports the Mesopotamian fashion of the third millennium BC: a bustled robe made of tufted wool.

of a divine ruler turned citizens' attention away from the dangers without to the glories within. What walls existed were for definition rather than for defense, and towns became open developments of dwellings around a central temple dedicated to the pharaoh or one of his sibling deities.

As in Mesopotamia, the temples were more than places of worship. As well as being centers of administration, from which the pharaoh's bureaucracy governed the surrounding countryside, the temples also acted as economic siphons, controlling, collecting, and counting the wealth produced by their citizens. Within their huge, walled enclosures stood offices, archives, storerooms, and living quarters for officials and priests. Their power was enormous: At the time of Ramses III in the twelfth century BC, his temple in the southern capital of Thebes controlled one-fifth of the nation's farmland, owned 400,000 head of cattle, and employed more than 86,000 people. Its wealth in silver, gold, and other precious metals was incalculable.

But if the temples sucked in the country's material wealth, they offered their citizens a good spiritual return on their investment, for the belief that preserving the body meant survival in the afterlife pervaded Egyptian religious thought. Even the poorest peasants mummified their dead in the desiccating sand of the desert. And if survival after death was important for such ordinary mortals, it was even more so for their god-king. Accordingly, the country's wealth, in labor, property, agricultural produce, minerals, and trade, was conveyed through the temples to one end: the building of a fitting tomb for the pharaoh. Egypt had become a nation of undertakers.

Along the Nile, huge pyramidal edifices and imposing rock-hewn chambers were

A vignette of everyday life in the fifteenth century BC, painted on the wall of an Egyptian vizier's tomb, depicts a gang of Nubian and Syrian laborers making mud bricks. In the lands of the Middle East, where timber and stone had to be brought from a distance, mud provided a cheap and readily available building material. Dug from the ground and loaded into baskets *(center)*, the mud was mixed with straw before being poured into molds *(upper right)* to bake in the sun. Once hardened, the bricks were removed and stacked ready for use *(upper left)*. Buildings built of mud rarely lasted long. But what the material lacked in durability it more than made up for in convenience: When a house disintegrated, it was a simple matter to mold bricks for a new one.

created to house the embalmed remains of successive pharaohs. Their construction demanded all that the temples could offer. The Great Pyramid of Khufu at Giza, for example, on which work started in 2575 BC, is estimated to have taken more than 100,000 men twenty years to build—an enormous diversion of human and material resources. Nor was it sufficient for the pharaoh to have just a tomb. In the hereafter, Egypt's rulers needed to live just as they had done in life, surrounded by their family, nobles, and retainers. As the tombs of Egypt's aristocracy gathered around those of their masters, the country became dotted with twin cities: one to house the dead and one to house the project's laborers.

The centralized endeavor that dominated the country left its stamp on urban construction. At the center of each city of the living stood an official royal complex, containing temples and palaces, as well as housing for the pharaoh, his family, the priesthood, and state officials such as the police chief and mayor. Outside sprawled the residential suburbs of the citizens, a mixture of rich and poor, but with those farthest from the center being reserved exclusively for workers.

In one city, Tell al-Amarna, a specially built capital erected midway between Memphis and Thebes in the fourteenth century BC by the pharaoh Akhenaton, the villas of the wealthy followed roughly the same plan: pillared reception halls, baths, and lavatories, plus luxurious family quarters, their surrounding gardens imaginatively laid out with terraces, pools, and decorative niches for statues. Elsewhere in the compound were accommodations for household servants, plus a kitchen and bakery.

The gap between rich and poor was great. But as an essential cog in the machinery for perpetuating the cult of the pharaoh, the lowly workers were not entirely neglected. The settlement at Deir el-Medina, for example, founded in 1500 BC in an isolated valley just outside Thebes, housed craftsmen specializing in the construction of royal tombs. As royal employees, these tomb builders enjoyed special privileges: Water was brought to them daily by teams of donkeys; they had their own fishermen to keep them supplied with fresh and dried fish from the Nile, and specially employed launderers to wash their clothes. Within an area of slightly more than one acre, a compound wall enclosed some seventy dwellings, laid out in straight terraces and separated by narrow alleys. The houses were long, narrow, and cramped, but far from slums. Each contained a hall, reception room, workshop, and bedroom. At the rear stood a courtyard kitchen, often with stairs down to a storage cellar.

Not all craftsmen were so favored. Many of the inhabitants of Egypt's cities would have been transient, seasonal workers. The massed labor required for tomb construction could only be freed from the fields between July and October, when the Nile's flooding made agricultural work impracticable. And the material from which the cities were made was as ephemeral as their occupants; although Egypt had access to huge natural deposits of stone, the quarried blocks were mainly reserved for temples and tombs. Dwellings of the wealthy might have the luxury of a stone door frame, or costly imported timber pillars, but otherwise they, like those of the less well off, were made entirely from mud brick. In time, they would all crumble to dust, leaving as sole monument to Egypt's glory the tombs of the pharaohs, whose scale was so immense as to defy destruction.

While Egypt's workers were toiling to raise tombs to their kings, another people far to the east were laboring to construct their own urban legacy. Like the ancient world's other civilizations, that of the Indus Valley prospered from the annual inundation of its river, whose rich deposits of alluvium yielded surplus crops for its farmers. In the middle of the third millennium BC, a growing cultural uniformity throughout the valley seems to have brought about the establishment of a central government, with its capital city probably at either Mohenjo-Daro, which lay near the mouth of the Indus, or at Harappa, situated about 350 miles to the north on a tributary, the Ravi.

It was a prosperous society, which thrived not only on agriculture but also on commerce. Major trading centers grew up to handle the lapis lazuli, turquoise, and metals from Afghanistan, Persia, and central Asia, which were trundled south by oxcart or donkey train to be transferred to ships bound for the Persian Gulf. At the same time, the Indus Valley towns developed their own exports, notably semiprecious stones and valuable hardwoods such as teak, cedar, and rosewood. So great was the flow of goods that on occasion Indian merchants had to set up permanent residence as trading agents in the cities of Mesopotamia.

While the necessity of organizing and maintaining irrigation systems had brought Egyptian and Mesopotamian societies together, citizens of the Indus were united by the river in a different fashion. The annual floods that gave the valley life also brought it destruction: Whole villages would have to be evacuated before the massive force of the Himalayan thaw, and occasionally, the river would change its course, bringing life to new areas but at the same time rendering old settlements obsolete. At the mouth of the Indus, the situation was complicated still further by earthquakes. On at least three occasions, a huge ridge of the earth's crust was thrown up, blocking the

To the accompaniment of harps, lyres, and reed pipes, defeated citizens march forth to greet their Assyrian conquerors. One of the fruits of civilization, music was initially deployed not for individual pleasure, but in the service of religion. But by the time this relief was carved in the seventh century BC, music was giving rhythm to the life of citizens as they marched to battle, danced at festivals, or joined in communal labor.

river's course. As the resultant lake increased in size, it reached back to all but engulf Mohenjo-Daro. Strong levees were constructed to hold back slight rises in water level. But when the full floods came, the only strategy was to retreat. While the Mesopotamians and Egyptians toiled to raise walls, tombs, and temples, the people of the Indus labored at a much more basic task: that of literally raising their civilization above the threatening floodwaters on huge mounds of earth and rubble.

Their efforts were not always successful: Disasters such as the one that occurred at Mohenjo-Daro were more than even the Indus engineers could cope with. But after every reversal, the citizens bent their backs to rebuilding their cities, brick for brick, exactly as they had been before. And the people of the Indus were nothing if not methodical. Weights and measures were standardized, baked bricks were of uniform size, and the 100 or so substantial towns in the valley were built according to a broadly similar plan.

At Harappa, for example, a central citadel was raised on a mound that stood forty feet above the plain, faced with a thick embankment of bricks to safeguard against erosion. Nor were the Harappans vigilant only against the forces of nature: A high, crenelated wall studded with towers topped the flood defenses. Within the citadel were crowded administrative offices, temples, and the residences of officials. To the north, meanwhile, on a slightly lower mound was the residential quarter, as much as 640 acres in area, laid out in straight parallel streets about thirty feet wide. Between these main arteries were large blocks of houses built of baked brick and divided by unplanned lanes onto which the entrances of the houses opened.

If the Harappans were threatened by water, they had at least learned how to live with it in the most effective way. A feature of the Indus Valley cities was the sophistication of their drainage systems. Many houses had shower rooms and toilets whose waste pipes discharged into dry wells or central sewers in the street. The sewers, which were maintained by a municipal authority, were roofed in with brick and provided with regularly spaced manholes for inspection and maintenance.

The people of the Indus Valley were not the only ones to struggle to overcome the might of a river. According to Chinese mythology, civilization arose in that country due to the activities of a leader named Shen Nung. It was he who instructed his people in the arts of agriculture and commerce, and also taught them the techniques of flood control. They had good need of the wisdom he imparted, because, from the fourth millennium BC, Chinese farmers had been congregating in villages around the course of the Yellow River in the north of the country. The river was well named. As it flowed down from the northern mountains, it carried with it huge quantities of the area's yellow soil, which colored both it and the Yellow Sea into which it ran. Not only did this cause erosion in the river's upper reaches, but in the lower stretches, the accumulated sediment caused the river to rise above the level of the surrounding plains. In times of flood, the river would burst its banks to cascade calamitously onto the farmers' fields and settlements.

Over the centuries, the combined necessities of tapping the river for irrigation and at the same time building dikes to battle the deluge had united the Chinese in a civilization that, by the middle of the third millennium BC, centered around a collection of well-fortified towns. Their society was highly stratified, ruled at the top level by hereditary kings, priests, and nobles. The priests were a vital prop of rulers because they were believed to have access to the spiritual universe from which they brought

wisdom and foreknowledge. Invested in the kings, this knowledge reinforced their authority to guide and command. At the bottom level were the peasants, who produced agricultural surpluses, acted as army conscripts, and provided unpaid labor on a huge scale for such public works as irrigation and flood control. In between was a growing class of specialists skilled in arts such as jade and bone carving, bronze smelting, and particularly fine ceramic work.

In the late third millennium BC, the northern regions of China were united under a single leader, Yu the Great, whose origins, according to legend, were inextricably linked with the river. In 2297 BC, after a particularly disastrous flood, Yu was charged with taming the waters. It took him and thousands of workers thirteen years of dredging and digging before the task was completed. The result was a placid river—which supposedly remained so for 1,600 years—that gained Yu the title of emperor.

What truth there is in the story of Yu will never be known, but if the legend is to be believed, it was while the Yellow River was still under his thrall that China's first recorded civilization began to emerge. For by the latter part of the second millennium BC, China's scribes were using ideograms to detail important events in civic life: court events, proclamations, treaties between noble factions, the lineage of clans, and historical events. Moreover, since about 1500 BC they had been working for definable masters: China's ruling Shang dynasty, who for some five centuries brought efficient government—as well as the intricacies of chariot warfare and an accurate calendar—to a centralized kingdom that embraced most of the tribal groups north of the Yangtze River.

Little remains of the Shang's urban achievements. The scribes who recorded their rulers' movements did so for the most part on perishable materials, and the cities themselves were built mostly of wood and earth. From the foundations of the settlements, however, it is possible to ascertain that the Shang not only moved their capital several times, but that each was built along similar lines: a high defensive wall, within which the city was divided into regular, rectangular blocks, at least one of which was an imposing palace enclosure that doubled as a religious center. The bulk of the population, meanwhile, lived outside the city walls in simple houses whose floors were sunk up to nine feet below ground level for insulation; in times of crisis, however, the people sought safety in the city.

The extent of the Shang's building operations was concrete testimony to their power. At one capital, Zhangzhou, for example, the thirty-foot-high city wall ran for more than four miles to enclose a rectangular area of 800 acres. The very building of such a defense would have been a monumental task. The wall was made of neither mud brick nor stone, but of earth, laid down in four-inch-deep layers between boards and compacted by the force of stamping feet. It has been estimated that to construct Zhangzhou's walls—which were sixty-five feet wide at the base—would have required the services of 10,000 laborers for twenty years.

There is no doubt that the wealth and manpower would have been available. Around the capital, for a distance of almost two miles, spread the mass of suburban villages that housed Zhangzhou's population. Manufacturing was carried out on a vast scale: One of Zhangzhou's many potteries comprised no fewer than fourteen kilns, while a single bronze foundry occupied an area of almost 10,800 square feet. And even if warfare occasionally disrupted production, the citizens of Zhangzhou were quick to turn it to profit: The city's bone workshop did a brisk trade in arrowheads and cups made from human skulls.

Compared to the unruly spread of huts and workshops outside its walls, Zhang-zhou's interior layout was a model of orderly planning. Its dwellings, probably wealthy residences, were laid out in a rectangular grid, while to the north there stood the palace—a long, timber-framed building, raised on a platform of tamped-down earth and equipped with a thatched roof for protection against the summer heat.

The pattern set by the Shang capitals was to provide the basis for urban growth in China over the following centuries. Ruling dynasties might occasionally be over-thrown—the Shang kings fell to a subject people, the Zhou, at the end of the second millennium BC—but no foreign invaders disturbed the evolution of Chinese civilization. Cocooned from outside influences, the walled cities grew in size and number over the centuries, ceremonial and administrative centers for an empire that, by the middle of the first millennium AD, was the most populous and wealthy in the world.

The achievements of the world's first citizens notwithstanding, their lives were still immutably bound to their agricultural origins. And in many cases, their downfall could be ascribed to the very rivers that had given them life.

For all the sophistication of the Indus Valley civilization, it suddenly disappeared in around 2000 BC. The exact reason for its demise is unknown, but one likely explanation is that the river, which the Indus peoples had battled so hard to subdue, finally got the better of them. At Mohenjo-Daro, for example, it was probably a shift

Great Plaza   Ball Court   Temple

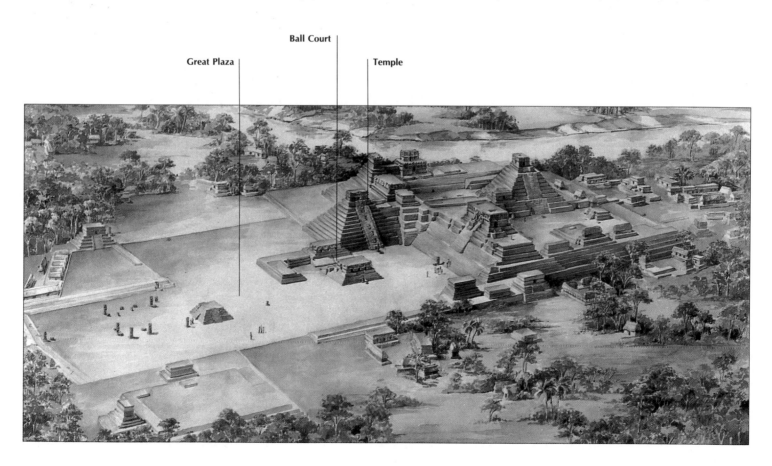

in the course of the Indus that turned fertile fields into desolate tracts. In other areas, denudation of natural forests to provide fuel for the baking of millions of bricks may have led to erosion, with the river reclaiming the valuable topsoil it had once deposited. Whatever the reasons, the once-proud civilization disintegrated into isolated agricultural settlements, many of its people drifting eastward across the Ganges watershed where a more lasting urban development was about to begin. Not until the mid-nineteenth century AD would Harappa's mighty brick edifices once again support civilization—as ballast for British India's Lahore-Multan Railway.

The downfall of the Indus civilization was felt as far afield as Mesopotamia. Deprived of one of its major trading partners, Ur dwindled in importance, and the center of civilization moved north to the city of Babylon. But a trade recession was just one factor in Ur's demise. Due to vagaries in the earth's climate, the water table in that area was steadily sinking. And the rivers that might once have come to the aid of Ur's farmers were now working against them. While opening up land for cultivation, the Sumerians' extensive network of irrigation canals was also steadily poisoning the fields. Waters that had once run deep were now spread over a multitude of shallow channels, and as they evaporated in the heat of the sun, they deposited residues of salt. As increased salinity rendered the soil unusable, so Ur became moribund. By the fourth century BC, it had been abandoned altogether.

Egypt as well lay at the mercy of its river. During the second millennium BC, a series of consistently low floods caused a period of famine, which devastated town and countryside alike. Agricultural yields plummeted as farmers turned to pastoralism rather than a settled farming existence. By the twelfth century BC, grain prices were soaring, and even the royal craftsmen were beginning to riot. In 1153 BC, the tomb builders at Deir el-Medina stopped work and approached a scribe to petition the pharaoh on their behalf: "We have come here driven by hunger and thirst. We have no clothes, no fat, no fish, no vegetables. Write this to the king, our good lord, so we may be given the means to live." Nor was it in foodstuffs alone that Egyptian citizens were feeling the pinch. Commerce was suffering, and an additional source of outrage for the temple artisans was that they were unable to get the oil with which all Egyptians were accustomed to clean themselves. Increasingly, as people sought desperately for the means to sustain themselves, state records began to detail the trials of tomb robbers rather than temple income. It was symptomatic of a deep malaise within the kingdom, and the rot was as evident to those without as to those within. In centuries to come, successive waves of invaders would sweep through Egypt, cannibalizing whatever remained of the kingdom's cities for their own purposes.

In 323 BC, however, one particular invader arrived whose coming signaled new hope for Egypt's—and the world's—cities. When Alexander the Great brought his Greek armies first to Egypt and then through Mesopotamia to the crumbling ruins of the Indus Valley, he brought with him the seeds of a new kind of civilization. In the years to come, it would be the classical stamp of the Mediterranean powers that would give new impetus to the rise of cities.

27

THE CLASSICAL ACHIEVEMENT

Few newcomers to Rome in the second century AD could fail to be impressed by the city's new Forum, or market complex, cut into the side of the Quirinal Hill. Along one side ran a huge, columned mall for food vendors, where the visitor could wander through long arcades of stalls on five floors, the air filled with a babble of voices as traders hawked their wares. Here was the cornucopian produce of an empire: grain, olive oil, fruit, vegetables, and wine from the Mediterranean countryside; exotic spices and peppers from the East; and, on the top floors, live fish that thrashed about in tanks filled with either fresh or salt water.

Opposite the mall, across the great marble-flagged area of the Forum, two libraries rose toward the heavens, containing all the accumulated learning of an expanding imperial power. Beside them stood a court of law that, with its spacious, shaded walkways, its elaborately designed pavements of inlaid marble, its ceilings glowing warmly with bronze tiles, and its walls lined with exquisitely sculpted marble statues and bas-reliefs, testified to the godlike force of Roman justice. And lest, amid this spectacular display of imperial and metropolitan pride, any beholder forget the individual whose beneficence had made it all possible, the center of the Forum was occupied by a giant equestrian statue of Emperor Trajan, while between the two libraries stood an imposing triumphal column, ornately carved with scenes of the emperor's great campaigns in eastern Europe and the Middle East—the booty from which had funded the new complex.

Trajan's Forum constituted just one impressive symbol of Rome's wealth and power. All over the rest of the city could be found other grandiose edifices testifying to Rome's position as capital of the greatest empire the world had ever seen. Here was money, fame, and political power—all of the magnetic attractions of a metropolis to which people flocked by the thousand.

Large cities were not a new phenomenon. Thousands of years earlier, mighty complexes such as Ur, in the Fertile Crescent of the Middle East, and Egypt's Thebes, on the lush banks of the Nile River, had brandished the glories of civilization before the inhabitants of the ancient world. But now their achievements had been surpassed. For the classical cities of the Mediterranean—of which Rome represented the apogee—had ushered in a new era of urban life, the influence of which would profoundly affect patterns of civilization up to the present day. Under the aegis of first the Greeks and then the Romans, the city became far more than just a cluster of buildings. It was an ideal, representing new forms of government and new ideas of citizenship: an ideal, moreover, that did not end at the edge of the built-up area, but embraced the surrounding terrain, of which the physical city formed merely the center. As the armies of each power spread outward, they brought with them the civilizing influences of the mother country. By the fifth century AD, the Romans

An imaginary cityscape painted in the first century BC shows the facades, porticoes, and balconies of urban dwellings interlocking as closely as the pieces of a jigsaw puzzle. Rome, the largest city of the classical world, became so densely packed that many of its leading citizens sought relief from its claustrophobic atmosphere by escaping when they could to country estates and villas. This painting adorned the bedroom wall of a Pompeian villa overlooking the Bay of Naples, an area that became the playground of the Roman rich until the eruption of Mount Vesuvius in AD 79.

29

An Athenian pottery ostracon dating from about 500 BC is inscribed with the names of candidates for ostracism, who were sent into exile for ten years.

Greek urban planning was guided by the same models of order and harmony to which all the other arts of Greek civilization aspired. Care was taken to ensure that cities blended with their environment, and random development beyond the city walls was limited. The distribution of buildings reflected the equal importance afforded by the Greeks to the private, public, and sacred spheres of life. And in keeping with the democratic principles of Greek politics—which allowed freeborn male citizens to elect their own government and to vote unpopular politicians out of office—rich and poor were spread throughout the city and enjoyed equal access to its facilities.

The Greek ideal was most fully realized in colonial cities built from scratch to house new settlers. Typical of these was Priene in western Asia Minor, shown on the left. Built on the southern slopes of Mount Mycale according to a grid pattern codified by the fifth-century BC architect Hippodamus, its six main streets were intersected by fifteen smaller arteries, many of them steep flights of steps. The focal point for the city's 4,000 residents was the agora, an open marketplace where people gathered not only to buy and sell but also to exchange news and gossip. Near the agora stood the bouleuterion, or council chamber, a fish and meat market, and a temple. To the north, overshadowing the theater, was a 650-foot-high cliff whose summit served as a citadel, while to the south lay the recreation area, including a gymnasium and a stadium.

1 Agora

2 Theater

3 Temple of Athena

4 Bouleuterion

5 Gymnasium

6 Stadium

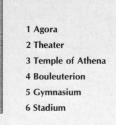

PRIENE: A COLONIAL MODEL

would seem to the Latin poet Rutilius Namatianus to have made a "city of the far-flung world." And indeed, despite the fact that most people still lived in the countryside, far removed from the nearest town, their lives were unlikely to remain wholly untouched by the institutions of their provincial center and, ultimately, those of their imperial capital. The city had become paramount, ruling the lives of all.

For the inhabitants of Greece, a thousand years before the birth of Christ, life was anything but city dominated. Far from being urban, Greek culture was entirely rural. Throughout much of the preceding millennium, Greece had been more or less united under the warlike rulers of Mycenae, a walled settlement that lay at the northeast corner of the Peloponnesian peninsula. By about 1000 BC, however, the warrior state had disintegrated, torn apart by internal rivalries and intrigue, and no comparable power had arisen to take its place.

Amid the shattered remnants of Mycenaean occupation, the Greek population lived dispersed throughout hundreds of tiny homestead settlements, sustained largely by the livestock they herded on their sparse hillside pastures. This peasantry was itself ruled and protected by local aristocratic warlords known as *basileis*. Despite his noble birth and warlike prowess, there was nothing very grand about either the status or the lifestyle of the *basileus*. Although a member of a larger ethnos, or blood tribe, he was a strictly local chieftain, presiding only over his *oikos*—the basic unit of Greek society, which included the lord, his wife, and their children plus a handful of dependent peasants and slaves.

All these people lived together, usually in a fortified hilltop house, around which spread the basileus' estate. Once their father was dead, the lord's sons parceled out his land equally among them, each establishing his own new oikos. Equitable though this arrangement may have been, it condemned all to a life of poverty, a struggle to make ends meet on inadequate, increasingly fragmented holdings of land.

The basileus, by and large, would have joined his people in impoverishment. He was not a full-time professional warrior; he was just as much a farmer, sharing with his peasants and slaves the heavy work on his land and, like them, depending upon its produce for his livelihood. War was, nonetheless, an essential part of life, at once a constant danger and an ever-beckoning opportunity. Where agriculture offered at best a hand-to-mouth existence, the booty of conflict provided a tempting way out of the cycle of poverty. And in time, some chieftains—bolder or perhaps more fortunate than their fellows—amassed fortunes. Around such prestigious figures, alliances were forged. This new spirit of cooperation eventually began to take physical form as the population increasingly built their dwellings around the strongholds of the great leaders. The era of the polis, or city-state, had arrived.

Like the fortified settlement from which it had grown, the new city was centered on a hilltop stronghold, or acropolis. But the people—freemen (the lords' families and dependents) and slaves alike—now lived outside the fortifications, in winding rows of sun-dried brick dwellings that huddled around the foot of the hill. The focal point of this lower town was the agora—a large open area where citizens would gather to talk and to trade. Symbolically placed immediately outside the gates of the fortress, the agora was the place at which the rulers met their subjects. It was here that the populace would assemble to hear the pronouncements of the council of elders, through whom the rulers came to govern the city. If the ordinary free people no longer lived with their lord, they had houses of their own; if their assemblies in the agora took place solely so that they might be informed of the decisions of their superiors, these meetings still gave them a role, however insignificant it might have been, in the political process. Gradually, despite the resistance they faced from the nobility, they would expand such assemblies' importance.

The development of the polis greatly increased Greece's prosperity. Farming remained the lifeblood of the Greek economy: The rise of the city did not lead to a decline in agriculture, but rather provided centers from which production in the surrounding countryside (always considered to be an essential part of the polis) could be organized more efficiently. Arable farming in the valleys was becoming increasingly important, supplementing the sheep and goat grazing earlier farmers had relied upon, and producing a surplus that could be used in trade. Greek settlements became important stops for the ships of the Phoenicians, the leading merchants of the time, who plied the Mediterranean Sea from their home ports in Lebanon.

This new wealth—far less dangerous to acquire than the spoils of war—brought with it dramatic changes to Greek society. The affluence of the nobles created a demand for luxury items such as decorative pottery, gold and silver jewelry, ivory ornaments, and elaborately wrought iron armor and weapons. Many of these could be manufactured by local artisans, but others—or at least the materials with which to make them—had to be imported. Profit-minded Greeks were quick to set themselves up as traders, either dealing with the Phoenicians or else shipping goods themselves in direct competition with them. Some succeeded; many others failed. Either way, people were finding alternatives to agricultural employment.

At the same time, wealth was beginning to move beyond the narrow boundaries of the nobility. The introduction of gold and silver coins—developed around 700 BC in Asia Minor—revolutionized the economy. No longer tied up in livestock and land, wealth could now be transferred from one individual to another with the utmost ease. Within the traditional ruling class, new inequalities and hierarchies were evolving, as some grew rich, while others remained poor, to be overtaken by opportunistic commoners. The power structures within society were changing. Wealth was beginning to displace birth and martial prowess as a measure of status.

This gradual redistribution of power was accelerated by a wave of colonization. Despite burgeoning agricultural output, good farming land was scarce, and Greek cities had little option but to look abroad for new pastures to feed their growing populations. In the eighth and seventh centuries BC, parties of young men set sail in search of space—first for the underpopulated hills of Asia Minor across the Aegean Sea, later for the West, where the coastal plains of Sicily and Italy offered rich land in abundance.

The settlements these colonists established took much the same physical form as the cities they had left. The central, raised acropolis, however, diminished in importance and, indeed, was often dispensed with altogether. Placed in an unfamiliar—if not downright hostile—environment far from home, these communities naturally tended to foster a spirit of collectivism. In such circumstances, it was inevitable that the agora, a space set aside specifically for public gathering, came increasingly to dominate civic life, and that the commoner's role became more important. Eventually, the shift in power spread back to Greece.

Ordinary people on the mainland had already begun to play a significant part in the defense of their cities, hitherto the exclusive province of the nobility and one of the main justifications of its authority. As early as 700 BC, a new type of military

Portrayed on a bowl from about 480 BC, sacrificial bulls are led to the slaughter. Usually, each animal was tethered in turn to a ring in the ground close to the altar and then dispatched by the priest with a single ax blow.

In this detail from a fifth-century-BC vase, a priest garlanded with laurel consigns the entrails of a sacrificial beast to the flames of the altar. He is helped by two assistants, also garlanded: One pours a libation; the other roasts meat for the feast to follow.

A sixth-century-BC vase shows four pentathletes—a jumper, a discus thrower, and two javelin throwers—preparing for action. Held to honor the gods, the pentathlon also included running and wrestling and became part of the Olympic Games.

The Greek love of grace and beauty is reflected in this bronze statuette of a veiled dancer made in the third century BC. Dancing, accompanied by the music of lyres and flutes, was often a part of festivals honoring the gods.

FESTIVALS OF THE GODS

For the city dwellers of ancient Greece, the best days of the year were the ones set aside for the worship of a particular deity. These festivals, or holy days—which became synonymous with holidays—were marked by processions, sacrifices, feasting, theatrical performances, and athletic contests. The Greeks conceived of their gods as larger-than-life humans, and it was assumed that what pleased humans would also please them.

The aim of the festivals was to win divine favor so that, for instance, the harvest would be abundant or a military campaign victorious. But they also helped to promote community spirit and brought color and excitement to the routine drudgery of people's daily lives. The Athenian leader Pericles boasted that "the contests and sacrifices throughout the year provide us with more relaxations from work than exists in any other city."

The start of every festival was marked by a grand procession—horsemen, charioteers, civic dignitaries, sacrificial animals, bearers of offerings—which paraded through streets lined with cheering spectators. After the procession came the animal sacrifices, usually carried out near an altar outside the temple of the god whose favor was being sought. The bloody ceremony was performed by priests, magistrates, and temple servants, to the accompaniment of flute music and the hymns of a choir. After a portion of each animal was burned on the altar as a meal for the deity, the remainder was then cooked and distributed to the worshipers, who welcomed the rare opportunity to eat meat.

formation, the hoplite phalanx, had been introduced. The heavily armed, rigorously drilled hoplites were Greece's first effective infantrymen. More important, they were also part-timers, ordinary freemen—farmers and craftsmen—who were making their own contribution to the protection of their city. While the nobility's warriors still formed a valuable cavalry force, their crucial importance as defenders of the polis was gradually ebbing away.

Increasingly, the city was claimed by the people. Once having undermined the dominance of the nobility in economic affairs and defense, the populace was now beginning to challenge the nobles' monopoly of government, and the institutions of civic life inevitably began to reflect the general social changes that had been taking place. Athens, which would ultimately prove the greatest of the Greek city-states, was a pioneer in the development of democracy.

Athens had been a polis since early in the first millennium BC, when the smaller settlements of the region of Attica combined to form a single unit. At the heart of the Athenian state, a city had grown up around a rocky acropolis overlooking the Saronic Gulf on the southeastern coast of Greece. Its sheltered coastal location made it a natural trading center, and from the eighth century BC, Athenian ships were plying much of the Mediterranean. Like those of the other Greek city-states, however, Athens's economy was based predominantly on agriculture. Conditions for Athenian farmers were harsh—those unable to meet the obligations imposed by the polis's noble rulers had their land confiscated and were enslaved.

In such circumstances, popular unrest was endemic, and in order to stave off revolt, the nobles were forced to make concessions. At the same time, as noble factions fought for power among themselves, they weakened their own position. Still further concessions were made to the populace to gain their support. And lavish programs of public building, undertaken for the same reason, served only to heighten the civic pride of ordinary Athenians.

In 507 BC, Athenian democracy came of age with the reforms of Cleisthenes. No idealist, Cleisthenes may have been just one more aristocrat looking to make short-term gains for his own clique. Whatever his intention, however, the governmental structures he introduced were dramatic in scope. All male Athenians—excluding the city's large number of slaves—now had the right to speak and vote at the city's assembly, the *ekklesia*. According to Cleisthenes' new constitution, both the 500-member council that governed the state and the bureaucracy that enacted its decrees were to be chosen by lot at the ekklesia from among all classes of free society. Their time would be paid for so that none would be prevented from exercising their rights because of financial need. Each day, lots were drawn by the council to find a president from among its members—for that day, the man appointed would be in charge, ruler of the city, presiding at the head of its council. The citizens of democratic Athens did not merely cast a vote at elections held every few years. They would almost certainly at some point in their lives hold public office, and they had the right to bring any issue before the full council of the city whenever they chose.

Despite these remarkable advantages, democratic Athens was never a utopia. In the fourth century BC, the philosopher Plato set the ideal number of citizens for the democratic polis at around 5,000. The population of Athens, however, soon surpassed this number, and its sheer size prohibited the full degree of participation that the constitution called for. While the population of the average Greek city-state was perhaps 1,250, only a few—the most notable of which were Sparta, Argos, Thebes, and Corinth—rivaled Athens, which, at its height in the mid-fifth century BC, had some 40,000 voting citizens. Including women, children, and foreigners—who enjoyed no political rights—the total free population of Athens approximated 150,000. There were, in addition, more than 100,000 slaves.

For democratic Athens was dependent upon slavery as apparently less enlightened times never had been. Slaves gave even the poorest citizens a sense of privileged status and, more practically, spared them demeaning types of work. A few independent-minded citizens recognized the injustice of the system. During the fifth century BC, the playwright Euripides wrote:

Slavery,
That thing of evil, by its nature evil,
Forcing submission from man to what
No man should yield to.

But his views won little support, even among intellectuals: A century later, the great philosopher Aristotle propounded the theory that people became slaves because they were naturally disposed to be servile. Certainly, the mass of common citizens, kept in comparative comfort and security, never questioned the fact that their political system subjugated huge numbers of people in far worse conditions than those from which they themselves had fought to escape.

Another brutal factor in the success of the Athenian state was warfare. Athens's redoubtable galley fleet was not only an important force in policing the Mediterranean, protecting Athenian trade, and bringing home slaves and other booty from foreign wars. It was also a major instrument of social control. "Must the ships be launched?" asks a character in a play by Aristophanes, an Athenian comic playwright of the fifth century BC. "The poor say yes," he goes on, "but the rich and the farmers say no." While the rich begrudged the money they had to pour into the war effort, and farmers feared the ravages of an invading army, the urban poor, who stood to earn extra money serving as oarsmen on the galleys, clamored for conflict. They got more than they bargained for.

War with a neighboring polis—a relatively frequent occurrence—was seen as a manageable and even welcome enterprise. But through the first part of the fifth century BC, the Greek cities were united against an expanding Persian empire. And in 480 BC, Athens's crushing defeat at the hands of the Persians led to the enemy's sacking the city and laying waste to the whole of Attica.

The destruction of Athens was an opportunity as well as a tragedy. The polis had become an abstraction, a spiritual idea greater than any collection of buildings. "You are yourselves the town," the defeated Athenian general Nicias told his shattered army, according to the historian Thucydides. "It is men that make the city, not the walls and ships without them." And over the succeeding decades, the people rallied around the project of reconstructing their city in its physical form.

Although unusual in its immense size, the Athens that was rebuilt through the middle decades of the fifth century BC was in appearance very much a typical polis of its time. As elsewhere, the trend toward popular power was reflected in the form of the city itself. Although the Acropolis was reconstructed in grand style, with a magnificent marble temple to Athena, the city's patron goddess, it was more civic ornament than fortress. As was the case in the colonies, the focus of the city had

An actor holds aloft his mask in this scene from a satyr play depicted on a vase of about 400 BC. In Greek theater, everyone wore colorful costumes and masks, and all roles were played by men.

These bronze tokens were used as admission tickets to Athens's Theater of Dionysus. The letters indicate in which section of the auditorium the ticket holders could sit.

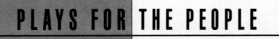

No casual entertainment, Greek theatrical performances were marked by a fervor that reflected their roots in rituals to honor Dionysus, the god of fertility and inspiration. By the fifth century BC, every Greek city had its theater, and every theater its full house. The focal point was the orchestra, a circular expanse of hard earth, often with an altar at its center, where the chorus and actors appeared. Behind this was the skene, originally a dressing room for the actors, whose projecting wings could be painted to represent a temple or a palace.

The auditorium rose around the orchestra in a semicircle that followed the natural contours of the landscape. The seats were originally temporary wooden benches, which were replaced by tiers of shallow stone seats whose hardness was alleviated by cushions brought by the spectators. The theater at Epidaurus, shown here, could hold an audience of 17,000, and its acoustics were so good that someone sitting on the top row could hear even the slightest murmur on the orchestra floor.

Programs were long and varied, and ranged from dark tragedies, telling of doomed heroes from the past, to comedies that lampooned famous figures of the present. Especially popular was the satyr play, a wild Dionysian burlesque performed by actors dressed as animals. A drama festival was a great democratic occasion, with local dignitaries rubbing elbows with the hoi polloi, even slaves and prisoners who were released on bail for the day. And it was free. For the state not only required its wealthier citizens to finance the productions; it also advanced the money to the spectators to pay for their seats.

Steeply banked tiers at the theater of Epidaurus in the northeast Peloponnesus, built in the fourth century BC, not only provided an uninterrupted view for every member of the audience but also enhanced the acoustics.

shifted down the hill to the agora, which was now the political, economic, and social center of the Athenian state.

There, an open, dusty, and largely unpaved area stretched out, punctuated by the occasional tree whose shade provided welcome relief from the midday sun. Eager traders hawked their wares among the knots of citizens who stood around chatting, discussing business, or playing dice. Around the agora's perimeter, meanwhile, other activities that had once taken place in the open air now had special buildings to house them. There was already a fountainhouse, built around a natural spring during the mid-sixth century BC to provide a convenient source of drinking water—always a precious commodity in the hot, dry climate of Greece—and, fortunately, left unscathed by the Persian invaders. Now this was joined by a bouleuterion, an enclosed building with semicircular rows of tiered seating to house the council meetings.

Another part of the square was roofed over to create a stoa, a colonnaded arcade that protected traders from the elements. The city's courthouse and the offices of the magistrates were also built around the agora, along with temples dedicated to important civic deities; later, a library was added.

But life for the Athenian was not just a matter of dry learning, administration, and trade. Democracy had spawned independence of mind and spirit as well as political liberty. Greek theater, which had originated as a religious rite, reached a peak of fluidity and expression in reborn Athens. During the annual Festival of Dionysus, citizens flocked to the theater—which held 15,000 spectators—on the south side of the Acropolis to see the great tragedies and comedies of the time. Here, on rows of seats that ranged up a natural slope, audiences enjoyed the offerings of Greece's dramatic giants—Aeschylus, Sophocles, Aristophanes, and Euripides.

The gymnasiums that sprang up around the city's outskirts were of equal importance to Athenian public life. There, under the cover of roofed colonnades, young men trained their minds in dispute with philosophers such as Socrates and Plato. Meanwhile, out in the courtyards, their fellows toned their bodies, running, boxing, or wrestling. For physical education was considered just as important as intellectual education. Every four years, Athenian athletes would join competitors from all over Greece at the Peloponnesian city of Olympia where, in 776 BC, a fleet-footed cook named Coroebus of Elis had sprinted to victory in the first recorded Olympic Games.

The spirit of inquiry and self-improvement that pervaded society was given tangible form in Athens's new public buildings. With their elegant columns and graceful symmetrical lines, these structures gave testimony to the serene confidence of the Greek city-state. Around them, for as far as the eye could see, sprawled the squat, often squalid homes of the populace. Yet, no matter how poor their own dwellings, the Athenians could still feel that they had a share in something majestic. As in other Greek cities, Athens's new fortifications were not constructed around the Acropolis, but in a long wall snaking around the

According to legend, Romulus, depicted on this silver coin, founded the city of Rome in 753 BC on the banks of the Tiber River. Rome's Latin-speaking inhabitants, however, soon fell under the influence of their powerful Etruscan neighbors, and it was not until 509 BC that they succeeded in expelling their Etruscan monarchs and establishing a republic. Tough, ruthless, and dedicated, they soon embarked on their own program of imperial expansion. "My Rome," Romulus is supposed to have said, "shall be the capital of the world."

city's perimeter—the homes and property of all were to be protected equally. Working on the reconstruction of Piraeus, the harbor district of Athens, during the mid-fifth century BC was a brilliant young architect from Miletus, a Greek colony in Asia Minor. This man, Hippodamus, was to give his name to a whole new system of town planning. It seems likely that the gridlike plan that Hippodamus perfected had evolved in the far-flung colonies of Greece, where the use of a regular standardized form enabled cities to be built quickly and without fuss. As applied by Hippodamus and his successors, this system, developed as a convenience, became an aesthetic triumph, enabling architects to give the city as a whole the symmetry and perfection of its public buildings. Within Greece, where plans that had evolved in older and less disciplined times still exerted an influence over the shape of the cities, it was not easy to implement; but overseas, Hippodamean planning rapidly came into its own.

For, with the final decades of the fourth century BC, another great wave of Greek colonization had begun. After Athens and the other great city-states had exhausted themselves in mutual conflict throughout the earlier part of the century, the rising power of the northern kingdom of Macedon finally became irresistible. Under the warrior-king Philip II and his son and successor, Alexander the Great, all Greece fell under Macedonian sway. A soldier like his father, Alexander had little regard for democracy, but he did admire the cultural fruits that the system had produced. Between 334 BC and his death in 323 BC, Alexander marched his victorious armies across the entire Middle East as far as Afghanistan and Asia, ushering in what would later become known as the Hellenistic age (after the Greeks' own name for themselves, Hellenes). Greek art, ideas, and town planning became the norm throughout much of the known world. And as Greek influence spread, new cities were established. Alexander himself founded some twenty cities named Alexandria in the course of his campaigns; the most famous of them, which stood at the mouth of the Nile River in Egypt, became one of the greatest cities of the ancient world.

The city-based life that Alexander had helped so much to promulgate thrived; but, for all the glories it had possessed, his empire did not. Barely a century following his death, the Hellenistic world had effectively dissolved amid a welter of dynastic struggles, economic division, and regional conflict. By that time, however, the torch of civilization had passed into new hands.

When, in 86 BC, the Roman general Lucius Sulla entered Athens, he did so to the accompaniment of the greatest bloodshed and worst destruction of private homes that the city had witnessed since the coming of the Persians. The power he represented was not, after all, one to knock politely on doors. Over the preceding seven centuries, Rome had steadily grown from a small settlement founded by the warlike Etruscan nation on the north bank of the Tiber River, not far from its mouth on Italy's west coast, into a well-disciplined and highly militaristic state whose empire encircled the entire Mediterranean. Greece itself had fallen to Rome in 146 BC, and rebellions, such as that which had now summoned Sulla's legions to Athens, were not to be punished with a mere slap on the hand.

Despite the ferocity of Sulla's arrival, however, it was significant that all of Athens's glorious public buildings survived unscathed—save one wooden structure that the Athenians tore down themselves to deny its timber to the invaders. For the Romans had long been acquainted with—and admiring of—the Greek civic model.

Since the first Greek traders had set foot in northern Italy, as early as the mid-eighth

The Arch of Constantine,
erected in the early fourth
century AD to mark the
emperor's victory over a
rival, is Rome's first monument of the Christian Era.

ROME: THE SPLENDOR AND THE SQUALOR

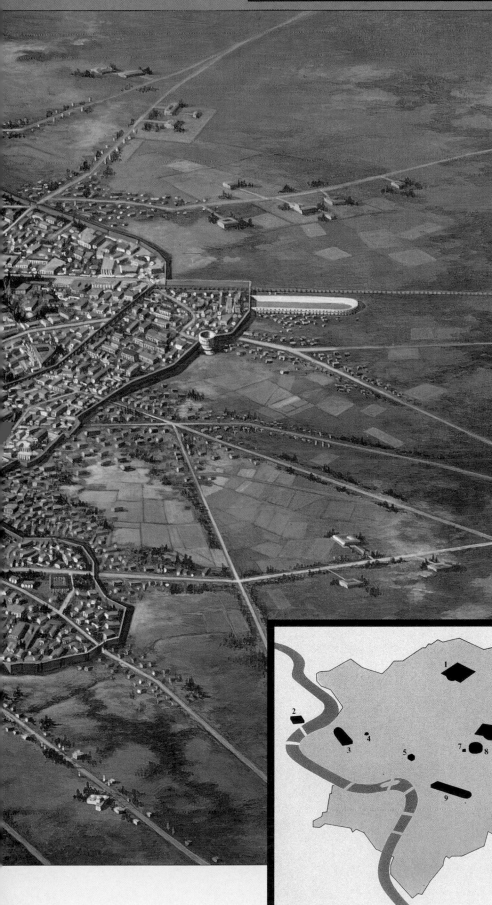

Rome, whose swollen population passed the figure of one million in the first century BC, broke all the rules of urban planning pioneered by the Greeks and applied by the Romans themselves to their colonial towns. Attempts were made repeatedly to impose order and control: Rome's water-supply system, for example, was the most advanced in the world, and after a great fire destroyed large areas of the city in AD 64, regulations decreed that new buildings should be constructed with fireproof materials and erected along wide, regular streets bordered by porticoes. But good intentions were nullified by a constant influx of immigrants from the provinces, most of whom lived in the chaos of narrow, trash-strewn streets and hastily constructed, fever-ridden tenements.

The dignity of the imperial capital was preserved only by the magnificence of its public buildings, which occupied almost half of the space available. The reconstruction on the left of Rome in the early fourth century AD shows some of the grandest edifices, which included temples, public baths, stadiums, and triumphal arches. Rome at this time was already in decline, having been supplanted by Constantinople as the empire's capital, but the monuments erected by successive emperors ensured that the legend of its glory would endure.

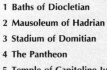

1 Baths of Diocletian
2 Mausoleum of Hadrian
3 Stadium of Domitian
4 The Pantheon
5 Temple of Capitoline Jupiter
6 Baths of Trajan
7 Arch of Constantine
8 The Colosseum
9 Circus Maximus
10 Baths of Caracalla

century BC, the Etruscans had been influenced by the emergent civilization to their east. And as the Romans embarked upon their campaigns of conquest, they constantly came upon more tangible proof of what that eastern civilization could achieve. They were impressed by the Greek settlements they encountered while conquering Italy, and even more so by the regular, logically organized Hippodamean cities they captured during their seizure of Hellenic territories around the Mediterranean. Here was an urban culture upon which they could build. And over the succeeding centuries, cities similar in their uniform grid plan to those of Greece, but bearing the unmistakable stamp of Roman occupation—a sobriety, discipline, and practicality that was far removed from the heady spirit of Greek society—would be erected throughout vast areas of Europe, North Africa, and Asia.

In this venture, the Romans were not just indulging in architectural banditry. The aesthetic attractions of the Hippodamean model dovetailed neatly with the precepts of their own religious tradition. Etruscan ritual decreed that a new settlement should be oriented strictly according to the four points of the compass and its rectangular perimeter marked out by a priest cutting a furrow with a bronze-bladed plow. From this trench, protective earth spirits would be unleashed at any enemy attempting to cross the city's boundary. Down through the centuries, the Romans remained influenced by such traditions, retaining the orientation used by their Etruscan forebears and keeping the tradition of the sacred furrow alive in the form of the *pomerium*—a strip of land around the perimeter of the city on which no buildings could be placed.

Administratively, too, the square grid plan made good sense. By their practice of "centuriation," the Romans divided up entire territories into equal, rectangular units of land, regimenting the countryside in the interest of uniformity and fairness of distribution among settlers. The regularly planned city, which the Romans and their Greek predecessors saw as being very much the center of the surrounding countryside, fitted well into this larger overall plan.

Indeed, it was the requirements of administration that lay behind the creation of many Roman centers. In order to subdue the territories they conquered, the Romans built cities wherever they went. Cities provided bases for the military personnel assigned to each region and formed staging posts along the great unswerving roads that ran from Rome to the distant frontiers. They also provided regional centers of government. Each region, or province, was under the overall control of a governor, appointed by and answerable to Rome. But within the province, every city had its own senate, a corporation of about 100 politicians and magistrates who undertook the daily running of the city—supervising the administration of justice, seeing to the maintenance of public buildings, organizing taxation, and making whatever decisions were necessary with a high level of autonomy. With administrative responsibility thus devolved from the center to the local governments in each city, the empire could be left, to a remarkable degree, to look after itself.

Civic life, moreover, literally "civilized" the Romans' wildest subjects. Agricola, the general who conquered Britain during the first century AD, was typical of the Roman leader who combined cultural with military imperialism. According to the historian Tacitus, writing shortly afterward, Agricola spent his first winter following the conquest encouraging Rome's British subjects to build temples and villas in the Roman style, and to adopt Roman ways. "As a result," wrote Tacitus, "the nation that used to reject the Latin language began to aspire to rhetoric; further, the wearing of our dress became a distinction, and the toga came into fashion, and, little by little, the Britons went astray into alluring vices: to the promenade, the bath, the well-appointed dinner table." Tacitus may have been more concerned with aggrandizing the achievements of Agricola than with giving an accurate account. But there could be little doubt as to the impact of Roman customs. As the historian noted: "The simple natives gave the name of 'culture' to this factor of their slavery."

The cities through which this insidious enslavement was imposed were substantially the same, whether founded on the windswept heaths of Britain or in the sunbaked deserts of North Africa. Minor local variations crept in as time went on, but the city was meant to embody Roman, not regional, values, and uniformity was prized. Built on a checkerboard street plan, with blocks of regular size (usually about one and one-third acres) and raised sidewalks for pedestrians, the standard Roman city had at its center an open market area, the forum, where citizens would meet to gossip and do business. Grouped around the forum were the city's official buildings, including government offices and the courthouse, while nearby, on a natural rise or artificial terrace, was the *capitolium,* the main temple, with separate chapels for the Romans' chief gods. And scattered through the public areas were monuments—statues of notable citizens, columns to deities, or triumphal arches—all helping inculcate a sense of pride in the city and in the empire as a whole. For entertainment, there would be an amphitheater for gladiatorial contests and possibly a smaller, separate theater for concerts and plays. After the forum and temple, the baths were perhaps the most important place for socializing in any Roman city. A complex of hot, tepid, and plunge pools, men went there to bathe or be massaged—or (despite repeated attempts to ban the practice) since bathing was often mixed, and the baths had a rather notorious reputation, to make assignations with prostitutes.

A floor mosaic from Rome's port of Ostia depicts an official measuring imported grain while laborers stand by with sacks of fresh supplies. The wheat and millet carried to Rome in ships from North Africa, Egypt, Sardinia, Sicily, Spain, and Gaul was inspected by the authorities and then either stored in warehouses or transported directly to Rome. To avoid riots due to food shortages, Rome's rulers made subsidized or free grain available to their citizens. On a set day of the month, people lined up at distribution points, presented their identity tokens, and received their rations.

While few private homes possessed any sanitary provisions other than basic earth privies, each city had its public lavatories, with long, communal ranks of seats, lined up either in semicircles or in rectangles, over troughs through which running water carried away the waste. Like the baths, the latrines acted as something of a social center: People would take their time over their visit and sit around chatting. Elsewhere in the city, there would be an enclosed public fountain, which gushed water that either came naturally straight from the ground or had been brought from some distance away by aqueduct.

A city with all these amenities was not built overnight, but the basic outline could be established within a few days of a legion's arrival, following standard military procedure for setting up camp. As the soldiers halted each evening of the campaign, they marked off a central point at which a burnt sacrifice would be offered to the earth spirits in order to ensure the success of the site. From there, they took sightings to establish a main east-west axis, and, from it, a north-south one, around which they set up their tents in a strict, rectangular grid formation. A stockade of upright wooden

The Colosseum, the largest and most famous of Roman amphitheaters, was inaugurated in AD 80 by the emperor Titus, who celebrated the occasion with 100 days of lavish and violent spectacle. The stadium could hold 50,000 spectators, who on hot days were protected from the sun's glare by a huge canvas canopy stretched on ropes across the top of the entire building. Admission was free, but seats were distributed according to social rank, those closest to the arena being reserved for senior dignitaries. The emperor, surrounded by his court, occupied the imperial box.

Horror and sensation spiced the spectacles that attracted the crowds on as many as 175 days of the year. The poet Juvenal complained in the first century AD that the Roman populace "longs eagerly for just two things—bread and circuses." Lasting from sunrise to sunset, a typical program included the killing of wild beasts—as shown above—and duels between gladiators. Jugglers and acrobats performed in the intervals between the main acts. On special occasions, the arena was flooded so that mock naval battles could be staged. In a single day during the inaugural festival, 5,000 animals were slaughtered; in a show held in AD 249 to commemorate the founding of Rome, 2,000 gladiators were paired off, and the animals killed included lions, tigers, leopards, elephants, hippopotamuses, and one rhinoceros.

In a fourth-century mosaic, gladiators do battle with spears, daggers, and tritons. The fate of those who were injured too badly to fight on was determined by the emperor or the host of the spectacle.

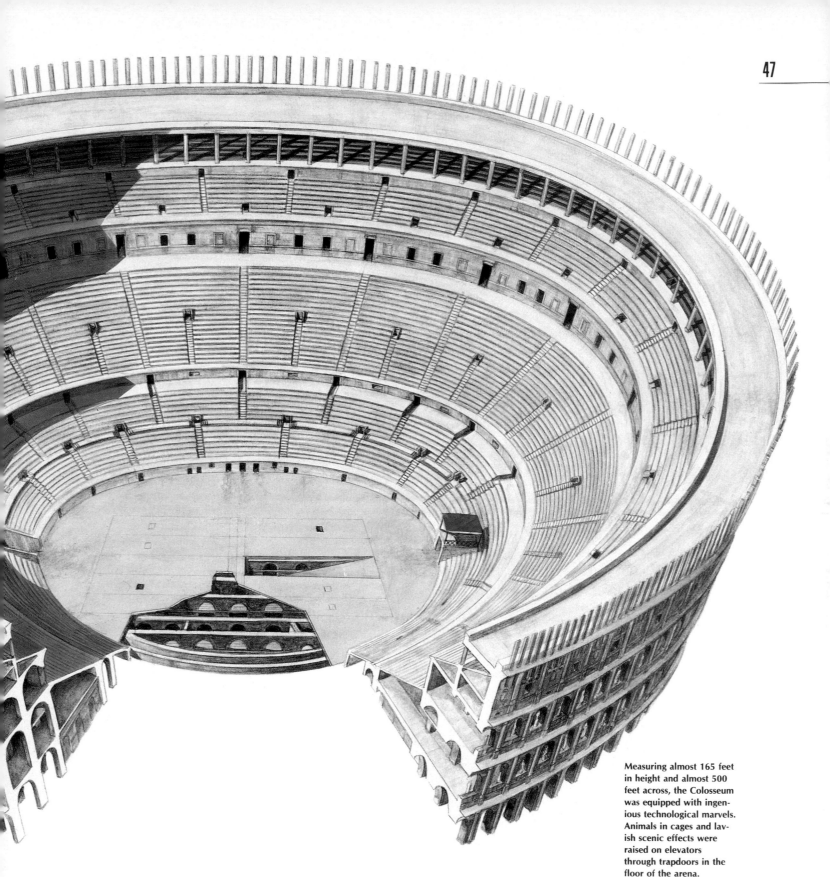

Measuring almost 165 feet in height and almost 500 feet across, the Colosseum was equipped with ingenious technological marvels. Animals in cages and lavish scenic effects were raised on elevators through trapdoors in the floor of the arena.

AN ARENA OF BLOOD

posts surrounded the whole, with a gate at each of the four compass points. Cities—many of them little more than permanent military camps—were built according to these principles, using more or less the same plan every time.

The Romans were not merely following a Greek model or an Etruscan tradition. The repetition of an established grid plan exploited the strengths of military discipline without requiring soldiers to understand the science of town planning. With such simple outlines to follow, soldiers could also make the most of native labor, which was plentiful but unskilled.

In addition to building these new cities, soldiers also formed their populations. Forbidden to have women accompany them during their periods of service, many kept wives and mistresses—often from among the local population—in houses outside the camp. After the legionary's term was up, he would simply lay down his arms and move in with his new family. Around the larger military centers, such as those at York in Britain, and Budapest in Hungary, a number of cities grew up in this way.

Not all such settlements emerged through happenstance. Some, designated as official colonies, made more formal use of the legionaries. Veterans were entitled to land as a reward for their services, but plots in Italy were scarce, and disgruntled farmers displaced to make way for retiring soldiers could become a potent cause of domestic unrest. Settling the veterans abroad provided a good return on Rome's investment, since they themselves would establish and govern the colonies, exacting tribute from surrounding territories and farming their allocated plots to make the land productive. Moreover, tough, campaign-seasoned former soldiers made ideal colonists for recently subjugated volatile areas. The practice also guarded against the possibility of rebellion by discontented veterans, giving them a limited share in the wealth of the empire while keeping them at a safe distance from the capital.

Whatever their origin, all Roman cities were consumer centers: There, the wealthy landowners of the surrounding agricultural estates lived, spending their profits. Smaller farmers came into the cities to sell their surplus produce and to buy essential goods. The city, thus, lived off the produce of its hinterland, its traders and artisans geared

This model of a multistory tenement complex, or *insula*—literally, "island"—at the port of Ostia shows the type of accommodations available to the common people of Rome. The spacious ground floor of such buildings was usually occupied by a rich tenant or by the landlord; the smaller rooms on the floors above were home to poorer families. Early timber-framed *insulae* were combustible and, according to the poet Juvenal, "shook with every wind that blew." The introduction of concrete, a Roman invention, in the second century AD gave added stability, but the inhabitants still lacked heat, running water, and sanitation facilities.

to meeting only local demands for goods. This did not make the city a mere parasite: The urban center provided the countryside with government and law, a market for its produce, and a link with the communications network that radiated from Rome.

Rome itself, intended to provide the civilizing model for a barbarous world, was, however, much more disorganized and haphazard than any of its satellites. In the same manner as a Greek polis, Rome had originally evolved around a hillside fortress. In about 600 BC, however, the swampy valley below the hill had been drained to produce a dry, level area that was to become Rome's Forum. There, a market town had grown up, oriented, according to tradition, around the four points of the compass. But no such religious confine could contain for long the mushrooming capital. For whereas the provincial cities remained relatively small and compact, there was a constant drift of people toward the center.

Standing in the same relationship to its mighty empire as one of its provincial cities did to its surrounding countryside, Rome acted as a magnet for the people of the entire ancient world. The richest landowners of the provinces came to Rome to spend their fortunes amid the best, most powerful, most fashionable society. Here, they gave extravagant public donations and private bribes in pursuit of the most lucrative political offices in the empire's bloated, top-heavy bureaucracy, or devoted themselves to the pleasures of the flesh at lavish banquets—with young slaves, both male and female, in constant attendance to complete the sensual experience. More and more, as members of the subject races won citizenship, Rome's ruling classes were of foreign origin, and tension grew as Roman patricians of one generation were overtaken by the new immigrants of the next. The poet Juvenal complained bitterly

A pair of wealthy customers attended by their slaves scrutinize a piece of cloth held by two shop assistants in this Roman relief dating from the first century AD. The shop's tiled roof and fluted columns topped with Corinthian capitals suggest that its prices would have been beyond the means of most ordinary citizens, who purchased their food and domestic goods from markets or single-room stores that opened directly onto the street.

WATER FOR THE CAPITAL

The office of chief administrator of the water department was hardly the most glamorous role in the Roman hierarchy, but as *curator aquarum* in the late first century AD, Sextus Julius Frontinus recognized that his work concerned "not merely the convenience but also the health and even the safety of the city." In addition to a white-collar staff of scribes and technical advisers, he controlled some 700 stonemasons, plasterers, plumbers, and other laborers. Leaks in the nine aqueducts that supplied Rome with fresh water from the surrounding hills kept these laborers working constantly, as did illegal attempts by private consumers to tap into the civic supplies. "The public watercourses are brought to a standstill by private citizens," complained standstill by private citizens," complained Frontinus, "just to water their gardens."

For most of their distance, the cement-lined channels that conducted water into Rome ran underground: Of the 270 miles of aqueduct administered by Frontinus, only about 40 miles were carried above-ground. Inside the city, the aqueducts fed into distribution tanks, from where myriad pipes led to public fountains and baths and the private houses of the wealthy. By a complex system of siphons, water was carried even to buildings on the Capitoline and other hills. Frontinus's stringent supervision enabled him to almost double the public supplies, and he was able to boast that "not even the waste water is lost": It was used to flush out sewers and public latrines before discharging into the Tiber River.

Aqueducts approaching Rome from the southeast bear water from five different sources: As the cutaway sections show, the aqueduct on the left carries two conduits, while on the right, three conduits are stacked above the arches.

The semicircular arrangement of this twelve-seat public latrine in a Roman town in Tunisia promoted social relaxation and conversation. In Rome itself, some latrines were adorned with marble seats and statues of gods.

This cast-bronze tableau of animals from a house in Pompeii was as functional as it was decorative: Water gushed from the mouths of the animals into a fountain basin.

in the first century AD of the cultural "sewage" of Syria and Greece pouring into the capital, drowning out the Roman way of life and upsetting the old social hierarchies.

The economic opportunities offered by the capital were great, and Rome's magnificence at its height during the first and second centuries AD could not be doubted. In the shadow of the Capitoline Hill, topped by the city's great temples, an awe-inspiring collection of public buildings had grown up. Impressive marble temples, courthouses, and government office complexes rose into the air, built to an astonishing pitch of symmetry and harmony according to principles that had been refined over the centuries from earlier Greek theories.

The wealthy endowers of these spectacular edifices—aristocratic politicians and emperors seeking either popularity in life or immortal renown in death—strove to outdo each other in terms of largesse and architectural grandeur. In the first century BC, for example, Julius Caesar had bequeathed his extensive private gardens across the Tiber to the people of the city as a public park and laid out a new forum at the foot of the Capitoline Hill. Over the ensuing decades, more open areas—such as that set aside by Trajan on the Quirinal Hill—were paved over and surrounded by new public buildings and colonnaded rows of shops to become new forums. Released from the confines of the original Forum—which by now had become the domain of financiers, moneylenders, and jewelers—other merchants were quick to move their stalls to the new marketplaces, extending the commercial heart of the city along with its administrative center.

Other public buildings bore witness to the growing importance of leisure in Roman life. The Colosseum, completed in AD 80, whose four stories of arched vaults supported tiered seating for some 50,000 spectators, was only one of Rome's many sporting venues. There and at other amphitheaters, shows were held to amuse the populace—convicted criminals and slaves fighting to the death in gladiatorial contests, animals massacred by the thousand by armed men or savage beasts—while at the Circus Maximus, hundreds of thousands of spectators gathered for the only slightly less gory thrills of the chariot races. Some stadiums could even be flooded with water, allowing imitation naval battles to take place. The shows were brutish but enormously popular. "Such a throng flocked to these shows," wrote the contemporary historian Suetonius, "that many strangers had to lodge in tents . . . pitched along the roads, and the press was often such that many were crushed to death." And their popularity was reflected in more than attendance alone. So great was the demand for novel or outlandish creatures to be slaughtered before the bloodthirsty crowds that whole species became extinct within the empire: The hippopotamus disappeared from Nubia, the lion from Mesopotamia, and the elephant from North Africa.

Other forms of recreation took a gentler tone. There were great theaters, as well as bathhouses, unrivaled throughout the empire. The latter's vast complexes contained not only a range of different baths—hot, cold, and lukewarm plunges, big pools for swimming, small tubs of hot water for soaking—but also areas for boxing, wrestling, and other sports; pleasant ornamental gardens fringed with shaded colonnades; stately esplanades where fine statues stood and cascading fountains played; and bustling arcades of shops. The great baths that were built by Emperor Caracalla in the third century AD comprised a network of business and entertainment facilities covering an area of more than thirty acres.

The physical infrastructure of the city at its height was impressive, but it was increasingly strained by a population that had, by the end of the first century BC,

CITIES MADE TO MEASURE

An aerial photograph of Timgad in Algeria, constructed in the second century AD, shows the checkerboard pattern of a Roman colonial city.

Following the example of the Greeks before them and making use of their soldiers' experience in setting up military camps, the Romans laid out the ground plans for new cities in their conquered territories according to a regular grid pattern. To ensure that the streets intersected at right angles, they employed a surveying instrument known as a groma, which consisted of a pivoting metal cross set on a brace that was attached to a pole. The pole was driven into the ground so that the center of the cross was directly above a peg marking the point at which two streets were to intersect; plumb lines attached to the ends of the cross were used to check that the pole was vertical. One bar of the cross was aligned with pegs marking the line of the street to be intersected. By sighting along the second bar, as shown in the illustration below, the surveyor could determine the correct position for a pole held by his assistant, and a line between the two poles could then be marked out. The same instrument was used to divide the surrounding countryside into regular homesites for new settlers.

reached about one million people—almost half of them slaves. Eleven aqueducts brought almost 300 million gallons of water a day into the city, according to one contemporary estimate. But only the very rich had water piped to their homes, and the majority of citizens were forced either to fetch their water from one of Rome's many fountains or else to buy highly dubious supplies from the city's water carriers. There were extensive sewers, superbly constructed (some big enough to drive a horse and cart through), but they were connected only to public drains and not to private houses, so they never even began to meet the real needs of the city. Most Romans used earth privies, public lavatories, or alleyways. Refuse—animal and human corps-

In this reconstruction of a street in Jerash in Jordan, Roman columns, pavilions, and paving identify the city as imperial property. During the second century AD, the Roman Empire reached its greatest extent, measuring some 2,500 miles from east to west and a similar distance from north to south. The provincial towns—from Timgad and Carthage in North Africa, to Antioch and Ephesus in Asia Minor, to Chester and Narbonne in northern Europe—though allowed only a limited degree of self-government, were endowed with the most sophisticated urban facilities available, including amphitheaters, public baths, and imposing arcades.

es along with other waste matter—was either simply left in the streets or dumped in great open pits, where it formed a rich source of disease. The stench of sewage, both indoors and out, was overpowering.

The characteristic grid plan that graced the Roman colonial centers was nowhere to be found within the imperial capital itself. Outside the grandeur of the city's imposing public areas, narrow, crooked streets were crowded with the multistory apartment buildings of the ordinary people. These *insulae*—or "islands"—could be attractive, neatly planned buildings, offering economical, relatively comfortable accommodations to middle-class families. More often than not, however, they were vertiginous, tottering structures, whose apartments would be sublet to numerous impoverished families. Some, rising as high as seventy feet, had the effect of completely blotting out the sun from the streets below. By the beginning of the fourth century AD, a survey revealed that there were more than 46,000 such buildings in the city. Between them, at intervals, could be found the light, airy, and relatively spacious private houses of the very rich, which were built facing inward around open courtyards, so that their blank, windowless outer walls formed an effective defense against the bustle and squalor of the city outside.

The streets were not only filthy but also overcrowded. Wheeled traffic, which was banned during the day by an imperial edict aimed at decreasing congestion in the city, traveled at night, filling the air with noise and making life all but impossible for the pedestrian—especially because the raised sidewalks insisted upon by law were, if they even existed at all, often blocked with merchants' stalls. During the day, it could be almost as bad, as pedestrians had to shove their way through the streets, being jostled by the sedan chairs of the rich—who may have kept their feet dry and clean but otherwise had to suffer a bumpy passage. Peddlers, beggars, and prostitutes competed volubly for customers, while snake charmers, magicians, and musicians, playing exotic instruments from every corner of the empire, further compounded the furor. Gangs of construction workers filled the streets with planks and other building materials, adding to the general din with their hammering and yelling. Drunks came lurching out of the taverns that were open at all hours on every street. Refuse thrown from upper windows and chunks of masonry falling from rickety tenements created an additional hazard. As Juvenal complained: "Anyone who goes out to dinner without making a will is a fool. You can suffer as many deaths as there are open windows to pass under."

Street crime was rampant—there was little to choose in murderousness between Rome's lower-class muggers and the gangs of aristocratic dandies who roamed the streets by night looking for violent excitement. Those who could afford it were carried about on litters and were accompanied by groups of armed bodyguards equipped with torches. The terror of attack was heightened by the very real fear of finding oneself hopelessly lost among the city's labyrinth of winding streets, unnamed and almost indistinguishable from one another in the dark.

For the very poor, life in the big city was wretched indeed. While many of those immigrants who came flocking to Rome found employment, thousands more did not. Those who failed—in the face of fierce competition—to find a living at their own trade faced a dismal future, since the city's menial work, which might otherwise have provided a safety net, was performed primarily by slave labor. By the first century BC, there was a significant underclass of the poor and idle, a volatile group that was always likely to break into disorder. As the mob increased steadily in size and ferocity through succeeding centuries, the authorities resorted to buying its docility by handing out free bread from public storehouses and staging ever more lavish gladiatorial contests and exhibitions for its entertainment.

Such was the wealth yielded by Rome's vast territories that the financial burden of the capital could be carried with relative ease—but only as long as Rome still possessed those territories. By the third century AD, the pressure of barbarian tribes around their periphery was beginning to take its toll. The cost of keeping the enemy at bay was staggering: By AD 220, the bounties being paid to barbarian chieftains to stop them from crossing the border equaled the entire army's payroll. And as the cost of defense grew, so the Roman economy deteriorated. Imperial treasures were sold, property confiscated, and the currency devalued in an effort to provide war revenues. Ever-higher taxes steadily impoverished cities and citizens alike, and at the same time, threw an increased burden on the state, which had to provide for the extra numbers of poor it had created. Inflation soared: The same measure of wheat that could have been bought for half a denarius in the second century AD commanded an official price of 100 in the third—and a black market price of 10,000. The Roman currency was leached of 90 percent of its silver, and in some Egyptian towns, bankers refused to handle it altogether. Everywhere, Roman prestige was collapsing.

In AD 293, faced with an increasingly unmanageable empire, Emperor Diocletian divided his domain into four separate parts. Inevitably, this move stripped Rome of much of its importance, and the growing power of the eastern regions was confirmed in AD 330, when Emperor Constantine established a new capital, Constantinople, on the site of what is now Istanbul.

In the decades to come, the Roman Empire was gradually but inexorably whittled away by invading tribes. From north and east, a stream of Germanic peoples—the Visigoths, Vandals, Franks, and Ostrogoths—pressed across the imperial borders, throwing the whole Roman world into confusion. By 378, the Visigoths had defeated the emperor deep inside his own territory. And thirty-two years afterward, the unthinkable happened: The Visigoths sacked Rome.

"The city that took captive the whole world has itself been captured," lamented the Christian monk Saint Jerome. Indeed, it must have seemed as if the whole world had turned on Rome. Through the centuries that followed, as successive tribes roamed at will through Italy and western Europe, Constantinople assumed the mantle once worn by Rome, as capital of an empire that still endured in the East.

But even that dominance was to be short-lived. Every winter, the citizens of Constantinople would draw their fur-trimmed coats close against the icy winds that swept in from the Balkans to freeze the Bosporus solid. Their actions were symbolic of their urban culture as a whole, for by the seventh century AD, Constantinople had withdrawn into itself to become the last cocoon of classical civilization. Beyond its walls, the glories of both Greece and Rome had all but vanished. The great cities, with all their commercial wealth, their ruling elites, their colonnaded magnificence, and, above all, the concepts of citizenship they had fostered, had become distant memories. In the West, barbarian tribes squatted amid the ruins of classical cities, their campfires the only light in a period that would become known as Europe's Dark Ages. In the East, meanwhile, the last outposts of imperial Rome had been submerged by a wave of Muslim warriors. As Europe struggled to emerge from the depths of its civic winter, it was in the warm lands of the Middle East that a new civilization would rise to leave its stamp on the world.

LIFE IN THE SHADOWS

In the world's great cities, from ancient Rome to modern Tokyo, respectable society has always existed hand and glove with its negative image: the shadowy underworld of criminals and malcontents who exploit the community around them. Like urban nomads, these social pariahs defy with their opportunism the order that defines city life. For them the city's ever-shifting population is the prey: The city's faceless anonymity gives perfect cover for the hunt, and its teeming streets provide an ideal sanctuary in times of danger.

This low-life world of villainy and illicit pleasure is the child of the very society it preys upon. Since city walls were first raised, they have enclosed areas of poverty and overcrowding—the perfect breeding ground for crime. In eighteenth-century London, for example, certain slum districts formed a criminal microcosm complete with its own rules and even its own secret language, or cant.

If the cause of the disease has remained constant through the ages, so have the symptoms. Prostitution is known with good reason as "the oldest profession": In classical times, a foot (above) imprinted on a pavement in the ancient Turkish city of Ephesus openly advertised the presence of

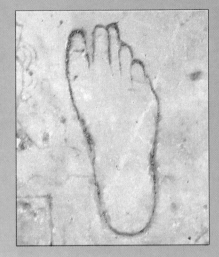

a brothel. The consumption of hashish and opium was as much condemned in medieval Cairo as in modern New York. Organized criminal societies such as the Chinese Triads and Sicilian Mafia flourished for centuries in their homelands before expanding into industrial cities worldwide.

For some, the underworld holds a perverse attraction: As one London peddler of broadsides told the Victorian chronicler Henry Mayhew, "There's nothing beats a stunning good murder after all." But to urban authorities it is an enemy as threatening as any outside aggressor.

The menace frequently has been met by the military: In the first century AD, for example, Rome was patrolled by three 1,000-strong squads of soldiers. More often, however, the suppression of crime lay in the hands of understaffed—and often corrupt—local constabulary. It was the late seventeenth century before the world's first professional police forces emerged to wage the endless war against crime.

PREDATOR AND PREY

In a 1788 painting entitled *The Westminster Election*, a young boy picks the pocket of a man distracted by the charms of an attractive woman.

For muggers, pickpockets, and other opportunistic criminals, the city streets offer rich pickings. Badly lighted roads, crowded public places, and narrow, winding alleys provide a perfect sphere of operations for these denizens of the underworld.

Some work alone; others run in gangs with a considerable degree of organization. As described in the cant of the eighteenth-century English criminal—or the *argot* of the French and the *Rotwelsch* of the German—the seemingly simple task of pick-pocketing became high art: The "foin," or pickpocket, might require the services of a "stall" to maneuver the victim into position, a "knuckle" to jostle him, and a "snap" to remove the spoils speedily from the scene. The operation has changed little to this day. And despite the possibility of police intervention, the modern victim might well have to resort to the same action as his eighteenth-century counterpart: the raising of a hue and cry to bring public-spirited citizens to his aid.

An unarmed citizen demonstrates how to overcome an assailant in an engraving from a 1674 Dutch manual on self-defense. The book was probably a response to the needs of a society unprotected by a police force.

A ratcatching dog is put through its paces before the gamblers at London's Blue Anchor Tavern in this mid-nineteenth-century painting. This sport created a huge demand for rats—a popular venue might stock 2,000 rodents at one time.

For jaded citizens with money to burn, the doors of the underworld's brothels and gambling houses have always stood open. Moralists have inveighed against the sex industry for centuries. The fourth-century Roman emperor Theodosius I condemned the Turkish city of Aphrodisias, where spectators surrounded an arena 575 feet long by 100 feet wide to ogle naked women cavorting knee-deep in water. In 1161, England's King Henry II tried to regulate what he described as the "orrible synne" by opening official bawdyhouses. And in 1687, King Louis XIV of France took a sterner tack: Brothelkeepers could be sentenced to having their noses and ears cut off. But to little avail. Even today, despite international attempts to suppress female exploitation, the "synne" prevails.

No less condemnation has been reserved for the destructive allure of the card table, the racecourse, and the dog track. And even greater outrage has been provoked when gambling combines with the sadism of bearbaiting, ratcatching, and cockfights.

Under the arcades of the Palais Royale, prostitutes vie for trade in a painting of 1809. As Paris's main leisure complex, the Palais offered living and business quarters for hundreds of so-called nymphs of joy.

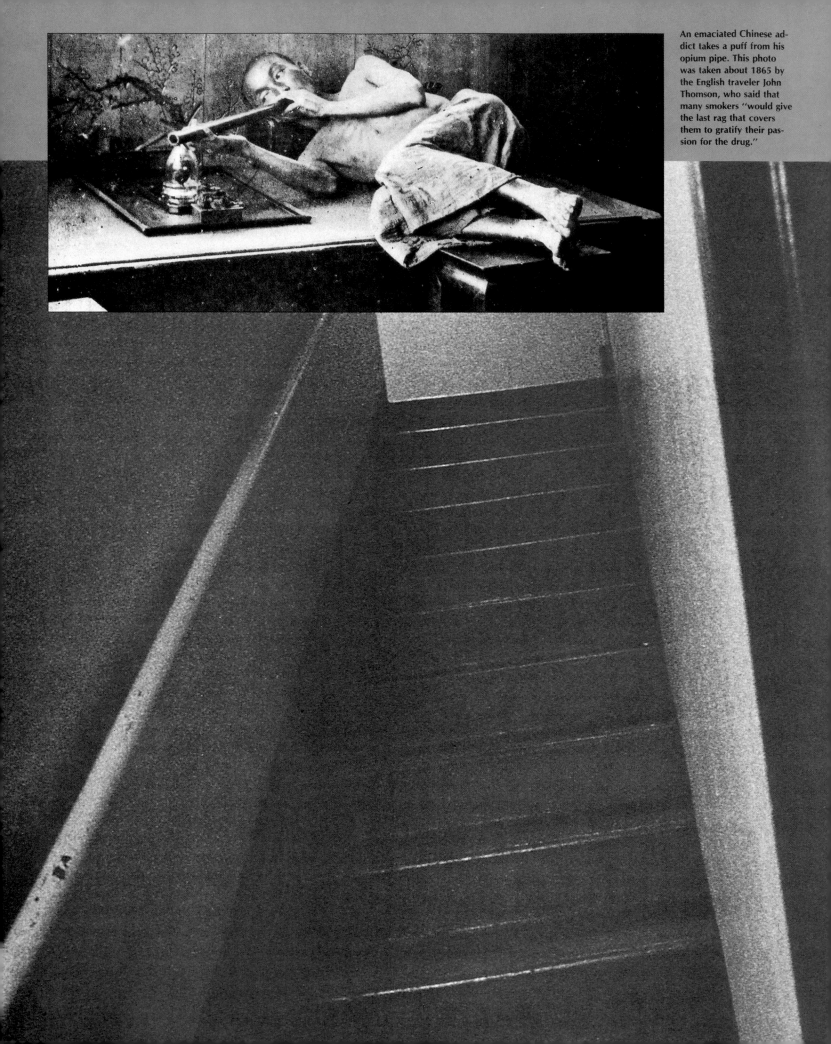

An emaciated Chinese addict takes a puff from his opium pipe. This photo was taken about 1865 by the English traveler John Thomson, who said that many smokers "would give the last rag that covers them to gratify their passion for the drug."

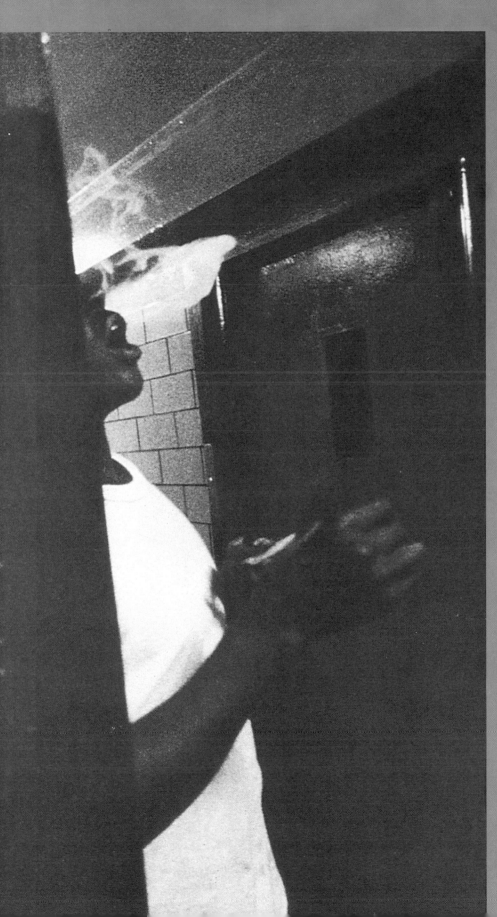

The temporary haze of pleasure provided by drugs and alcohol has made them time-honored props for those wishing to escape the miseries of urban life. "Drink until you are drunk," urged the caption to one Egyptian painting in the second century BC. "Spend your day in happiness!" But the effect has often been exactly the opposite. When cheap gin flooded the London market in the first half of the eighteenth century, it had dire consequences. By 1743, eight million gallons were being consumed; one gin shop on Holborn Hill reportedly served more than 1,400 customers in three hours. The spread of vice, poverty, and violent crime was universally attributed to the easy availability of alcohol.

In the industrial world, the trade in social oblivion reached staggering proportions. The economy and health of nineteenth-century China was shattered by massive imports of opium from British India. And today, the wealth of drug barons in places such as Colombia derives directly from inner-city misery as Western addicts resort to crime to pay for their expensive, self-destructive habit.

Gin Lane, a 1751 engraving by the English artist William Hogarth, depicts the horrific effects of gin drinking on London's poor. By 1742, with churches recording twice as many burials as baptisms, the phrase "dead drunk" held real meaning.

THE ORIENT ASCENDANT

If the Arab general Amr ibn al-Ās had been looking for a blood-stirring battle, his latest conquest was a disappointment. In AD 642, he reported back to his leader, "I have taken a city of which I can only say that it contains 4,000 palaces, 4,000 baths, 400 theaters, 1,200 fruit and vegetable vendors, and 40,000 Jews." The great Egyptian port of Alexandria, erstwhile pride of the classical world and jewel of the eastern Roman Empire, had surrendered without a fight.

All around the eastern and southern fringes of the Mediterranean Sea, the same thing was occurring. In a steady succession, the outposts of imperial Rome were falling—with greater or lesser degrees of bloodshed—to invading Arab armies from the desert peninsula of Hejaz. The demise of the western half of the Roman Empire had begun in the fifth century with invasions by the barbarian tribes of Europe. Now, two centuries later, the Arabs were finishing off classical civilization in the East. But whereas in Europe the Fall of Rome had led to the decline of urban life, the cities of the Middle East and Asia continued to flourish. Under the banner of Islam, the old classical settlements were transformed into thriving centers of trade, learning, and commerce, distinctively modeled according to the demands of their new masters.

Farther east the ancient civilization of China, virtually untouched by the world beyond its western boundaries, was to encompass some of the largest and grandest cities the globe had ever seen. It would be many centuries before a resurgent West caught up with the achievements of its eastern neighbors.

By the time Amr's forces marched into Alexandria, the Eastern Roman, or Byzantine, Empire—centered in Constantinople—was already threatened. Costly wars with neighboring Sāsānian Persia had severely damaged the economy of the eastern Mediterranean, and in the provinces of Syria and Egypt, citizens became estranged from an imperial government that offered them ever less in the way of military protection or economic benefits. As outlying cities drifted away from the influence of Constantinople, they came to be run by local notables rather than by imperial edict.

Bereft of central control, some imperial outposts decayed, and many were abandoned altogether. Great Levantine cities such as Caesarea, Petra, and Palmyra dwindled into ghost towns. Brigandage and raiding by local tribes were potent agents of depopulation, while plague was a regular and debilitating scourge: Few who had lived through it were likely to forget the epidemic of AD 541 to 544, at the peak of which there were 10,000 deaths a day in Constantinople alone.

Even in those cities that continued to flourish—such as Damascus, Aleppo, and Antioch—the demise of classical civilization was becoming visible. No longer kept clear by civic regulations, the wide thoroughfares, flanked by monumental public buildings, turned into warrenlike jumbles of houses pierced by twisting, narrow

Crammed between the mosque at far left and the mausoleum of the sixteenth-century sultan Qānsūh al-Ghurī (*near left*), Cairo's silk merchants ply a relaxed trade in an 1849 lithograph by David Roberts. The rents that the shopkeepers paid for their stalls—little more than narrow wooden booths fronted by stone slabs that doubled as benches and display counters—went to support the great religious foundations in whose shadow they traded. By day, the market was shaded by a lofty wooden roof; by night it was lighted by lamps, suspended from the mosque and mausoleum portals, which also illuminated the crowds of homeless poor who slept on the steps of the buildings.

Scattered throughout Asia, North Africa, Spain, and the Middle East, Islamic cities grew up as secretive honeycombs of the faith. Although the seat of urban government was a walled citadel, the lifeblood of any town pulsed mostly through its mosques, hammams, or bathhouses, and covered markets called suks. Around these communal centers swarmed an intricate maze of narrow streets within which were concealed myriad quarters, segregated not by walls but by race, craft, and religion.

In this stylized view of sixteenth-century Aleppo in northern Syria, a heavily fortified citadel dominates the densely packed surrounding buildings, which are themselves enclosed by a wall. Almost a town within a town, the citadel contained a palace, a mosque, a barracks, an arsenal, and large cisterns for collecting water.

By the time this illustration first appeared in a manuscript describing a Turkish sultan's campaigns, Aleppo's sturdy outer walls enclosed a population of more than 100,000. Mosques and suks proliferated throughout the city, their minarets and domes rising amid the citizens' one-story, flat-roofed houses. With every need catered to locally, it was possible for inhabitants of Aleppo (or any other great Middle Eastern city) to live and die in their own quarter without ever leaving it.

Houses were built back to back, separated by streets that were sometimes little more than three feet wide. And, apart from a military parade ground in front of the citadel, there were few open spaces within the city walls. But outside, there were orchards, gardens, and racetracks for the citizens' pleasure.

ALEPPO: A CITADEL OF THE FAITH

streets. Shops encroached on the avenues, the upper stories of residences were built to overhang the streets, and roads were blocked by new buildings. Private enterprise had become king, and if the neighbors did not protest, no one else would interfere. Besides, many saw positive advantages in the new confusion: In terms of personal comfort, narrow streets provided more shade; and, strategically, they were easier to close off and defend in times of external attack or internal riot.

There were also economic reasons for favoring a labyrinthine street plan. Throughout the eastern Mediterranean, camels and other pack animals were replacing wheeled traffic for the transportation of goods. The camel was a cheaper and more efficient carrier of goods than the oxcart; and if beasts were being used, then it was no longer necessary to maintain streets at the former high standards and width.

It was into this idiosyncratic urban world that the Muslim Arabs burst in the 630s while engaged in a holy war to expand the frontiers of Islam. The invaders were almost unstoppable. Their campaigns were carefully planned and coordinated, and their soldiers were highly motivated: Not only did they fight to acquire plunder and territory in this life, but should they die in the struggle, they would gain—according to the tenets of their religion—paradise in the next. By AD 637, the Arabs had occupied Persia and Iraq and had marched into the Byzantine city of Damascus. They stopped short of taking Constantinople, but in the ensuing decades, Egypt, North Africa, part of India, and most of Spain fell under the sway of the warriors of the faith.

Although its fighting men may have come from the desert, Islam was essentially an urban religion, first preached and practiced by the prophet Muhammad in the cities of Mecca and Medina. Its teachings advocated both a communal spirit and a strict preservation of privacy, which in some cases virtually amounted to a civic code: According to the Prophet, for example, a householder had the right to attach a beam to the outer wall of a neighbor's dwelling but not to overlook a neighbor's courtyard. Thus, when the armies of Islam swept out of the Arabian Peninsula on their trajectories of conquest, the victors did not disperse themselves in the countryside to become rural landlords. Instead they preferred to settle, with their families and retinues, where they felt most at home: in towns.

The newcomers imposed themselves on existing populations as an alien aristocracy, often underlining their dominance by building brand-new settlements outside the subject towns themselves. But initially, they made few changes in the way cities were run. Muslim conquerors were tolerant of different religions, and the taxes they imposed were less oppressive than those of previous regimes.

The most obvious change was the introduction of a new faith. Life in any Islamic town, whether old or new, was centered around a mosque—either one of the many *masjids,* small structures serving a particular locality, or the *jami,* the religious focal point of the city. In addition to offering spiritual solace, the mosques provided a forum for practical matters. Their airy, spacious interiors served as public offices where political issues could be debated, where new decrees and taxes were publicized, and where the community's treasury might be located. Here, experts in Islamic law delivered opinions on contentious issues and taught informally both religious and secular subjects. And from the minarets of every mosque, the muezzin called the faithful to their five daily prayers, his voice defining the sections of the working day.

Outside the mosque, there were usually a fountain and basin in which lesser ritual ablutions could be performed; and a hammam, or bathhouse, was built nearby for the performance of more thorough cleansing before going in to pray. Although the

A covered fountain dominates the courtyard of Cairo's Ibn Tūlūn Mosque. Built in the late ninth century, the mosque was Cairo's first jami. By the fifteenth century, the expanding city boasted 130 such structures.

Three arches and a mosque lamp are woven into a sixteenth-century prayer rug. Islamic ritual required not only kneeling but also prostration. Mosques often contained rugs that accommodated whole lines of worshipers.

Intricate carving adorns a fourteenth-century Koran stand. The stand was more than decorative: Extravagant volumes, given as pious bequests, could be so heavy that two men were needed to carry them.

THE HOUSE OF ISLAM

The pivot of Islamic civilization was the mosque. Every city contained at least one *jami,* or main mosque, that along with smaller structures called *masjids* served the needs of outer districts. Five times daily, men—women were encouraged to pray at home—came to prostrate themselves in prayer on the carpeted floor of their local mosques; and on Fridays, it was their duty to attend the jami, where the noon prayer was read in the name of the caliph.

At its simplest, the mosque was a flat-roofed enclosure for worship. There was little furniture, save for perhaps a Koran stand, used to support the holy text during public recitations and teaching, and a *minbar,* or pulpit, from which the sermon was preached. The mihrab, a niche toward which the congregation prayed, was set in-to one wall to indicate the direction of Mecca. In its fullest form, however, the mosque comprised a domed prayer hall, complete with open courtyard, and a min-aret from which the faithful were called to prayer. In addition, it might also include schools, orphanages, monastic cells, and other charitable institutions. On Fridays, the mosque's boundaries could spread be-yond its walls, as congregations overflowed into the streets.

Purity was an integral part of worship: Shoes had to be removed at the mosque entrance, and ritual ablutions were per-formed at a nearby basin or fountain. In times of drought, symbolic cleansing, using sand, was permitted.

A mihrab indicates the direction of Mecca on the eastern wall of Cairo's Sultan Hassan Mosque. As befits its importance, the niche is richly decorated with a pattern of inter-locking marbles.

hammam played a key part in the religious life of the city, it was also a place for
relaxation, gossip, and sexual assignations. And on cold winter nights, the baths'
furnaces—whose smoke was often a major source of air pollution— provided a cozy
haven for poor vagrants.

If the area around the mosque was an Islamic city's religious and social hub, the
nearby suk, or covered market, was its commercial heart, around which the residential districts clustered. For the Muslims were no strangers to trade. Encouraged by
the teachings of Muhammad to go on pilgrimages to Mecca, they saw no harm in
making the trips profitable. Caravansaries—hotels-cum-warehouses, several stories
high and built around a central courtyard—sprang up on the outskirts of every city
to accommodate merchants, their goods, and their animals.

From the caravansaries, the fruits of the traders' travels would be taken to their final
point of sale, the teeming, clamorous suk. Here were shops and workshops of every
description, each grouped by craft into separate streets or quarters—all the shoe-
makers in one street, all the metalworkers in another, and so on. It was a natural
move. The clustering of like with like allowed shopkeepers and artisans to combine
to defend their interests; at the same time, it made it easy for the shopper to compare
price and quality. There was no strict rule about this segregation: A street occupied
by sellers of almond sweetmeats might well contain the workshop of a leather-bottle
maker. But there was a tendency for the sellers of books, prayer beads, and incense
to have their shops near the mosques, where they could catch the trade of the pious.
And smelly or noisy industries, such as slaughterhouses and dyehouses, were usually
located on the edge of a city, if not outside the walls themselves.

Islamic cities did not grow in an orderly fashion. They expanded, rather, in patches
of humanity. To distance themselves from their subjects, rulers commonly built their
palaces outside the old city, thus creating a separate civic nucleus. And as newcomers came to settle in the city, they formed their own quarters on the outskirts,
distinguished by race or religion, and centered on new groupings of mosques, suks,
and hammams. In this way, the Islamic city came to be a honeycomb of individual
units, each a part of the whole, yet retaining its own distinct characteristics.

Not all growth was so haphazard. Although theoretically united under a single
political and religious leader, the caliph, the Islamic conquerors were subject to
internal rivalries and power struggles, acknowledging the caliph's temporal position

only where his armies made it necessary. Frequently, a dynastic ruler or military leader would decree that a planned city be built from scratch. Such cities served both as centers of government and as advertisements for the political and military successes of the dynasties concerned. Some grew to vast size; others were hardly more than large palace enclosures. But when the ruler lost control of the city or moved to another site, the buildings fell into ruin through neglect, and local interests and private pressures combined to erase all traces of the leader's grand design.

One such city was Baghdad, founded in AD 762 by the caliph Abū Jafar al-Mansūr of the Abbāsid family as the capital of the Arab empire. The site, formerly a summer camp of the Sāsānian emperors of Persia, was well chosen, lying beyond the reach of the Abbāsids' western rival, the Fatimids, and near their supporters in the eastern area of Khorāsān. Equally important, Baghdad was located on the Tigris River, and a network of canals linked it with the Euphrates, which, like the Tigris, emptied into the Persian Gulf. Shipborne trade was vital to Baghdad. Within half a century, the city's population had risen to almost one-half million, a number it was impossible to feed from the immediate agricultural hinterland or by supplies brought cumbersomely and expensively overland. As al-Mansūr remarked of Baghdad, "This is the Tigris; here is no distance between us and China. Everything on the seas can come to us."

The building of Baghdad took just four years. It was a new foundation, a planned city with streets and buildings laid out on formal principles. According to the ninth-century essayist al-Jāhiz, "It is as if it were poured into a mold and cast." The round wall enclosing al-Mansūr's capital was pierced at regular intervals by four gates, from which roads ran in toward the center, dividing the city into four quarters. Different sectors were reserved for the residences of functionaries, such as the palace guard, the water carriers, and the muezzins. Where the roads converged stood the caliph's palace, known as the Golden Gate from its imposing gilded entrance. This splendid gateway and the long sequence of antechambers culminating in the caliphal throne room effectively intimidated and impressed foreign embassies. Early Arab historians even reported that the golden dome of the caliph's palace was topped by an automaton, a mounted warrior who pointed his lance in whichever direction military danger threatened. The Golden Gate stood at the symbolic center of an Islamic universe.

Al-Mansūr's round city was not vast—possibly only six-tenths of a mile in diameter—and even before its completion, suburbs were being built outside the walls. Like the sectors within the city, these suburbs became earmarked for different types of inhabitants. That of Al-Karkh, for example, grew up initially to house the workers required to build the city (later, it became the main commercial zone of Baghdad); that of Al-Harbiyya, to the north, was chiefly settled by al-Mansūr's soldiers.

Built around an open courtyard, the sixteenth-century Qānsūh al-Ghurī caravansary in Cairo (below) provided storage and stabling for animals at first- and second-story level, while the rooms above offered accommodations for traders and sometimes for long-term lodgers and billeted soldiers. Such urban depots served as hostels, warehouses, strongrooms, and trade centers for wholesale merchants. In the countryside, a network of caravansaries, such as the one below (inset) in a seventeenth-century manuscript, were constructed as staging areas for merchants plying between the great trading cities of the Islamic world.

For all the glories of al-Mansūr's palace, Baghdad's days—and those of its caliphs—were numbered. By AD 935, the Abbāsids had been reduced to figureheads kept in gilded captivity by Persian and Turkish warlords who rarely bothered to visit the city. Finally, in 1258, Mongol horsemen from central Asia invaded Iraq and took Baghdad. The city was sacked, its citizens were massacred, and the last Abbāsid caliph of Baghdad was wrapped up in a carpet and trampled to death by Mongol cavalry. In the centuries to come, Baghdad would be rebuilt many times, but it would never regain its former splendor. By the fourteenth century, the seat of the caliphate had moved to the Egyptian capital of Cairo.

Founded in AD 969 by the Fatimid Muslims of North Africa, Cairo had originated as a planned city along lines similar to Baghdad. Situated just northeast of a town called Al-Fustāt—meaning "tent" in Arabic, as befitted a settlement that had grown from a military camp set up in 642 by the Arab general Amr ibn al-Ās—Cairo got off to an unlucky start. Astrologers were consulted about a favorable time to begin digging the foundations. But a passing raven set the signal bells ringing prematurely, and work commenced when the wrong planet was in the ascendant. Al-Qāhirah, the Arabic name for Cairo, means the "victorious"—a name that was chosen because, thanks to the importunate raven, the new city was created under the inauspicious dominance of Mars.

As originally planned by the Fatimids, Cairo was laid out on a formal grid pattern. As centuries passed, however, and dynasties rose and fell, that design disappeared. The streets were overbuilt, new settlements sprang up beyond the walls, and Fatimid masonry was plundered for other buildings. In 1171, a new seat of government, the citadel, was built to the south of the Fatimid city. Gradually, the space between this new limestone structure and the old city was filled in, and by the time the Mamlūk sultans—a dynasty of Turkish warriors—seized power in AD 1250, Cairo was spilling out in all directions.

Cairo's growth was not the result of a natural increase in population. The birthrate of medieval city dwellers was not high, and plague took a regular toll of those who survived to adulthood. Rather, Cairo's expansion, like that of most cities of the time, was fueled by immigration: peasants seeking their fortune in the city and foreign soldiers flocking to Egypt to sell their services to the sultan.

Not all of the newcomers came in search of money. Many of the pious and the scholarly were attracted by the prestige of Egypt's teaching colleges, the madrasahs—religious institutions of higher education that often adjoined a mosque. Primarily, professors taught the Koran, the traditions concerning the Prophet, theology, and religious law. Many madrasahs, however, also offered informal instruction in philosophy, history, astronomy, and alchemy. Scholars traveled between cities in search of reputable masters who could teach them what they wanted to know and who could grant them a diploma certifying their knowledge of a specific subject or text.

By the fourteenth century, Cairo had become a sprawling mass of streets, which hid a population of possibly 600,000. Not all of the city was inhabited at the same time: Some areas were deserted as others grew more fashionable; houses in which a murder had been committed were customarily abandoned; and a few places were shunned as the haunts of jinn, or ghosts. All the same, there could be no doubt that medieval Cairo was one of the largest cities in the Middle East. Anyone looking north from the citadel over the city would have seen a vista of minarets, domes, and towers reaching as far as the limits of vision. Ibn Khaldūn, the fourteenth-century philosopher-historian, declared, "He who has not seen Cairo does not know the grandeur of Islam. It is the metropolis of the universe, the garden of the world, the anthill of the human species."

At the apex of the anthill stood the sultan's residence, the citadel. (Although the new, Mamlūk-appointed caliph lent his prestigious presence to the city, he was, like his predecessors in Baghdad, little more than a puppet.) Here, Cairo's ruler received foreign ambassadors and distinguished visitors and, twice weekly, heard petitions from his subjects. Within the citadel's walls were housed the sultan's personal garrison of white Turkish slave soldiers. Outside were markets supplying horses and arms to the troops. There was also a large open space used for military parades and polo matches; the sultan played twice a week at noon, on Tuesdays and Saturdays.

Like most medieval Islamic cities, Cairo lacked autonomous institutions, and the senior civic authorities were personally appointed by the sultan. Paramount among these was the *wali,* or the military governor, whose police force fought crime—with greater or lesser degrees of enthusiasm, for they were notoriously corrupt—supervised curfews, shop-opening times, and public health regulations, and sometimes assisted in the collection of unpopular taxes. At night, the wali's patrols roamed the streets, paying particular attention to disreputable areas—among them the taverns (usually run by Christians, to whom the Islamic prohibition on alcohol did not apply), the hashish dens, and the *futuwwa* lodges—young men's clubs that had a reputation for violence and gangsterism. The wali also employed a comprehensive network of spies, who, shrouded in black hoods to avoid recognition, kept their ears open in the markets and shadowed suspicious foreigners, reporting back to the citadel.

The responsibility for trying and condemning criminals fell to a religious judge. But it was the wali and his agents who administered the penalties—a duty in which they had a wide scope. Besides imprisonment, exemplary punishments such as beheadings, bisections, garrotings, and crucifixions were common. The authorities, moreover, were keen to advertise the fate of miscreants. Prisoners were expected to pay for their food, but, since few had the means to do so, it was a common sight to see a chain gang of convicts with outstretched bowls snaking down the streets begging for their sustenance. Public executions took place at Bab al-Zuweyla, the southern gate of the old Fatimid city, which was spiked with the heads of the convicted. And those who had been crucified were sometimes paraded through the city, nailed to their crosses on the backs of padding camels. The public responded enthusiastically to this free entertainment: When, in the early fourteenth century, the unpopular Emir Qusun was condemned to death, lollipops in the shape of his crucified image were available from market stalls.

The trades, crafts, and marketplaces were supervised by an official called the *muhtasib,* some of whose functions overlapped those of the wali. The muhtasib, who was sometimes a civilian and sometimes a soldier, endeavored to enforce the provisions of Islamic law regarding overpricing, sales frauds, adulterated goods, short measure, and the like. However, his jurisdiction ran wider than that: He was the guardian of public morality, the scourge of scantily dressed women, trysting lovers,

and drunks. The muhtasib also employed those who served the city as night watchmen, torch-bearers, town criers, executioners, scavengers, carrion removers, and cesspit emptiers.

In theory, the muhtasib was responsible for the fabric of the city, with powers to widen streets or order the demolition of dangerous structures. In reality, however, he lacked the means to have much effect on town planning or to keep public utilities in working order, because Cairo, like other Islamic cities, was expanding along the lines of least resistance. Despite a ruling that streets be at least wide enough to accommodate two loaded pack animals, they rapidly became blocked with booths and stalls, which in turn grew into rough dwellings. Almost half of Cairo's streets now came to a dead end. One Persian traveler of the eleventh century had noted that the alleys of Al-Fustāt were so narrow that they had to be lighted even at noon. The few improvements the muhtasib was able to effect often contributed to the confusion. For example, sewers that were covered with flat slabs to facilitate maintenance were built alongside the main streets. As new buildings forced a change in their course, however, even these had to be constantly redug. And because the roads were regularly resurfaced with crushed limestone, its gradual accumulation caused street levels to rise steadily, turning ground-floor rooms into basements.

But not all urban maintenance was left in the hands of the muhtasib. Islam actively encouraged charity, and sultans and wealthy merchants alike would set aside income from their property—rural estates, shops, caravansaries, or industries—to support civic and religious institutions. The larger madrasahs often supported orphanages, hostels for the poor, and other worthy causes.

One such beneficiary was Cairo's Mansuri Hospital, a converted palace opened by the sultan Qalāwūn in 1284. Although many Arab cities boasted hospitals, the Mansuri was undoubtedly the most splendid and the most generously endowed. Its wards were divided according to sex and types of disease. Koran readers moved through the wards, providing edification and consolation for the sick and dying. In addition to the wards, there were a mosque, dispensary, library, lecture theater, and living accommodations for the doctors. Treatment was free and available to all, with preference given to the poor. There was nothing to match it in the world.

The street that the hospital faced, the Qasaba, could accommodate a dozen men riding abreast and was lined with mosques and the homes of the wealthy. But apart from this main thoroughfare, the Fatimid grid layout of streets had vanished. Behind

In this scene from a fifteenth-century Persian manuscript, a hammam attendant hauls down towels for his customers before they proceed to be bathed and shampooed. In addition to their washing facilities, most hammams offered massage and osteopathy to their clients. They were also places of recreation and gossip, especially for women, whose outings to the hammam might be their only escape from home. Occasionally, a rich lady would hire a hammam and invite her friends to a day of idleness surrounded by slaves and singing girls.

the Qasaba lurked the densely populated, mazelike quarters of goldsmiths, perfumers, slave merchants, carpenters, and other artisans. Cairo was the preeminent center of Middle Eastern commerce. Bulaq, Cairo's port on the Nile, was a staging area for international trade that came overland from the Red Sea en route to Alexandria or one of the other Mediterranean ports. It was also the place where grain from Upper Egypt and the Nile Delta was unloaded to feed Cairo's teeming population.

Off the broad highways that led in toward the central markets, meanwhile, clustered the residential streets of Cairo—narrow, densely packed alleys that often ended in culs-de-sac. And as with the trades, so with the people: Like tended to cluster with like. Thus, immigrants from Syria, North Africa, and elsewhere tended to live next to one another, as did Jews with Jews and Christians with Christians. Some wealthy merchants and generals maintained mansions in their own salubrious area, but in general, the quarters were not divided by income or class; thus, rich and poor lived cheek by jowl.

A typical dwelling was built around a courtyard, often with a fountain at its center. On the ground floor or the one above, there was a reception room, ventilated by a wind tower—a tall, projecting edifice, slatted with vertical vents that drew cooling breezes down into the building. Few rooms had fixed functions, but a strict Muslim ensured that a large part of his house was inaccessible to male guests and was reserved for the women, who could be visited only by the immediate family or by other female guests. For many women, the weekly trip to the hammam was their only day out. (Most hammams reserved three days a week for women's use.)

Not everyone who lived in medieval Cairo lived in a house. Few European visitors failed to comment on the vast numbers who slept out in the streets or who lived in makeshift tents or in holes in the ground. Indeed, for all the narrow streets and cloistered privacy of Islamic cities, life was lived mainly in the open air. Instead of going to restaurants, for example, it was the custom to buy and eat cooked food from pushcarts and stalls in the streets. And open spaces—even the grisly area before Cairo's Bab al-Zuweyla—were a positive magnet for street entertainers.

Here could be found the full gamut of performers, beggars, and exhibitionists—snake charmers, animal trainers, fencing masters, acrobats, tightrope walkers, low-grade prostitutes (distinguished by their red leather trousers), astrologers, and sword swallowers. Amid the mob rose the tents of the shadow plays, which presented bawdy, lowlife farces and satires to the accompaniment of musical commentaries. And striving to be heard above the din were professional storytellers, who recited popular romances or epic poems about Islamic heroes.

Meanwhile, down some side alley might be found a wrestling match, half-obscured by the group of eager spectators whose money was riding on the outcome.

A poetry debate enlivens the bookish milieu of a public library in a Mamlūk illustration to al-Harīrī's twelfth-century prose masterpiece, the *Māqāmat*. Usually attached to a mosque and funded by charitable endowments, Islamic libraries served as lively centers of study where local and visiting scholars would gather to exchange views. In addition, they housed workshops for scribes who toiled to copy the manuscripts that were stored flat in niches around the library walls. Not all of the works were scholarly: Books on the stratagems of robbers and cheats, for example, constituted a popular genre in Arabic literature. And in big towns, scribes sometimes offered lending services to customers in search of light reading.

Officially forbidden in Islam, gambling was nevertheless very much part of city life. There were even astrologers who specialized in guiding gamblers as to where their stakes were best placed. People placed bets on almost anything: on cockfights and other animal contests, and even on how long a man could stand on one leg—a "sport" that was lengthily and disapprovingly discussed by Islamic jurists.

Despite such amusements, life in Cairo was as dangerous as in any other large city. Fires were frequent—often caused by spontaneous combustion in the sultan's granaries—and in the absence of any official fire department, their extinction depended solely on local initiative. The aftermath of a large conflagration could be as damaging as the flames themselves: Popular opinion was quick to find a scapegoat in imaginary Jewish or Christian arsonists, often resulting in massive riots and pogroms.

Crime, too, was rampant—despite the attentions of the wali—and villains tended to gather in certain areas much like traders. Indeed, they even gained a certain measure of romantic respectability: Some of Cairo's more cunning criminals acquired a cult status that was celebrated in popular tales. The thief, for example, was widely hailed as *sahib al-layl,* or the "master of the night."

Not all wrongdoers were public darlings. There were large criminal gangs, often more than forty strong, whose members were capable of such outrages as smashing up markets or breaking into the hammams on women's day and raping the customers. And in times of severe famine, body snatchers appeared, who disinterred the recently buried and murdered people in order to sell the carved-up bodies as meat on the streets. Nor were the authorities much better: It was widely known that many of the police were criminals who had purchased their positions only to further their nefarious interests; and shopkeepers and landlords lived in terror of the frequent riots that took place between the sultan's white soldiers and their black grooms and slaves.

Cairo's size made it exceptional, but in most other respects, it was a typical Islamic city. Similar centers, complete with mosques, citadels, caravansaries, and muhtasibs, existed all over the Muslim world, from Fès and Córdoba in the West to Herāt and Delhi in the East. Rarely did they possess urban autonomy or have powerful guilds. The Islamic city was not a breeding ground for social change, and there was little evolution in its social forms. Cairo at the end of the eighteenth century, for example, was little different from Cairo in the middle of the fourteenth century—and the same held true for most other Muslim cities. They served their inhabitants well; and it was not until the advent of the industrial era that they began to follow the path of their Western counterparts.

If the Muslims felt no need to change their cities, then neither did the Chinese. By the Middle Ages, China's cities—some containing one million people—were already of a size and complexity to equal those of an industrial world that was centuries distant. The reason for this urban growth lay partly in the centralization of agricultural trade—in China, rural markets were few, and the bulk of large-scale commerce was conducted in the city. A history of financial sophistication had also spurred mercantile enterprise—since the eighth century, letters of credit, known as "flying money," had helped wealth circulate rapidly within the Chinese empire; and by the eleventh century, paper money was being used. But perhaps the greatest boost to a city's size was the presence of the ruling emperor. A vast bureaucracy was required to govern the world's largest and most populous nation, and every year, thousands of ambitious students flocked to the capital to take the prestigious civil-service examinations.

Set between hedges of myrtle, jets of water play over a stone aqueduct in the Genaralife, the summer palace of the Spanish sultans of Grenada. The desert warriors who spearheaded the Islamic conquests brought with them a traditional reverence for water that found solid expression in their cities. In addition to using water to adorn their own courtyards and gardens, Muslim rulers constructed cisterns, fountains, dams, and aqueducts for the benefit of their citizens. In medieval Samarkand, each house was supplied with piped water, which traveled across the town's open spaces in lead channels supported by wooden props.

One such shrine to ambition was Changan in central China, seat of the Tang emperors from the early seventh century AD. Its outer walls, more than sixteen feet high, enclosed an area of almost thirty square miles, in which, by AD 700, were packed the dwellings of more than one million citizens. And unlike the cities of Islam, Changan was carefully planned and ordered. According to Chinese theories about the cosmos, the ideal city was to be laid out on a grid plan and bisected by a central avenue, which ran northward to where the emperor's palace stood along with the offices and residences of his court and bureaucracy. The north-south axis was believed to channel supernatural forces in a way that would benefit the inhabitants of the city; the emperor, meanwhile, looked south from his palace, his protective back turned toward the north from where barbarian invasions tended to come.

Changan was truly a terrestrial city modeled on a celestial ideal. The central thoroughfare, lined with trees and drainage ditches, was wide enough to accommodate twelve carriages running abreast—and even the side streets could handle four carriages. The palace, meanwhile, was walled off from the outer administrative quarters, which in turn were contained within their own enclosure. Throughout the rest of the city ran walls, separating one quarter from another, to create a checkerboard grid of boxes within boxes.

When the Tang dynasty was overthrown in the late tenth century, the mighty capital sank back into the earth; for Changan, like all Chinese cities of the time, was built mostly of perishable materials—bamboo, wood, and mud bricks. But if the materials disintegrated, the concept survived. Hangzhou, eastern capital of the Sung emperors between AD 1138 and 1279, was built according to the same cosmological grid. When Hangzhou was superseded by the northern city of Beijing, that city too acquired the characteristic square shape under imperial direction. Even cities in countries as far afield as Korea and Japan followed the ideal expressed by Changan.

For all their structure, Chinese cities were far from placid. Their wide avenues were invariably packed with food stalls, horses, camels, donkey carts, sedan chairs, heavily laden coolies, and banners advertising goods and services, over which loomed the tile roofs and wooden balconies of inns, hotels, and shops. Beijing's densely packed streets were astonishing. A Spaniard who visited the place in the sixteenth century remarked, "Throw a grain of corn into the air and it will not fall to the ground." Foreign visitors were also struck by the noise. For Beijing, like all Chinese cities, was driven by bells and gongs. Temple gongs marked the times of the day, gave weather reports, and also warned of disasters such as fire. Even at night, the streets were patrolled by watchmen, who waved rattles to give audible proof of their presence.

Much of this commotion was directed toward profit. For commerce was the lifeblood of the Chinese city, and within its walls could be found an almost endless supply of goods. According to the thirteenth-century novel *Account of the Gruel Dream,* the interested purchaser in Hangzhou could find:

> . . . *early rice, late rice, new-milled rice, winter-husked rice, first-quality white rice, medium-quality white rice, lotus-pink rice, yellow-eared rice, rice on the stalk, ordinary rice, glutinous rice, ordinary yellow rice, short-stalked rice, pink rice, yellow rice, and old rice.*

In the big cities, the same sort of choice applied to almost anything—ivory combs, children's toys, lacquerwork, restaurants, and prostitutes.

A sixteenth-century silk scroll *(right)*, captures the southward-facing Forbidden City, or palace enclosure, of Beijing, just one of many Chinese cities laid out on geomantic principles. Geomancers, who studied the invisible forces that were believed to flow through the world, used compasses such as the one shown above to pronounce the most auspicious layout for buildings. South was the ritually favored point of the compass, and wherever possible, buildings were constructed facing in that direction. Geomancers were in constant demand by architects, town planners, gravediggers, landscape gardeners, and interior designers alike. They were sometimes even called upon to realign the bed of an ailing patient or the desk of a lackluster student.

The organizing force behind this plenty was the guild. Guilds acted as closed shops and employment agencies, allocated work among their members, and enforced minimum standards of craftsmanship. They also acted as benevolent societies, looking after the families of members who had fallen on hard times. There were an amazing variety of guilds—those for makers of small bells, for astrologers, scavengers, trimmers of kingfishers' feathers, and water carriers. There was even a guild for the blind, with its own officers, including a blind executioner.

Guilds also organized convivial dinners for their members. For, despite having only one day's rest in ten, medieval Chinese cities were far from work dominated. On festival days, there was jousting from riverboats, fireworks displays, polo matches (a craze imported from the Muslim world), and shadow-play theaters (a fashion that spread in the other direction). Cultivated people took days off to view the spring blossoms; more mundane pleasures included visits to teahouses and conversation with the courtesans who were to be found there, as well as trips to taverns where rice wine was served. Gambling was widespread, ranging from board games, such as mah-jongg (in which the players set out the pieces to re-create in miniature the ideal, square, walled city), to cricket fights. Moreover, there were societies such as sports clubs and poetry groups to assist the citizens in their pursuit of pleasure.

In general, Chinese cities may have been pleasant places in which to live, but they also had their squalid side. Municipal sanitation was a matter of private enterprise and, thus, often atrocious. The inhabitants of a street had to band together to pay a road sweeper. Similarly, household excrement was collected by entrepreneurs with buckets, some of whom made fortunes in the fertilizer trade. Moreover, although a few main streets were paved, the majority were simply dirt, and clouds of dust were thrown up by the passing streams of humanity. This miasma, intensified by the grime from household coal fires, hung around the city in a pall from which there was little escape—few buildings were more than one story high, those that were being the palace and temple pagodas.

The city air was not clean, nor was it free. The emperor was the biggest urban landlord. And, similar to the planning of their cities, Chinese rulers exercised strict control over the lives of their subjects. Markets were closely supervised and were restricted to certain designated areas within which the various crafts were allotted set places. The guilds were occasionally forced to provide loans, and they usually were obliged to sell their products at artificially low prices to the state. And although the use of paper money was a private business innovation, the imperial government soon stepped in to control its issue and circulation, rapidly becoming the major moneylender of the nation.

The state gave as well as took away. Imperial funding for hospitals and medical publications made the Chinese health service highly sophisticated. Nevertheless, it remained impotent in the face of epidemics. The bubonic plague, since called the Black Death, which swept the known world in the fourteenth century, proba-

Modeled in glazed pottery, an oxcart—and its two handlers—typifies the vehicles that streamed daily into Tang China's capital, Changan. During the seventh and eighth centuries AD, the Tang emperors maintained a network of canals and roads—many of them surfaced with stone and brick—which attracted goods, people, and ideas to the city. But even this solid infrastructure failed to keep pace with the needs of Changan's burgeoning population. Despite frequent bumper harvests, the city was often crippled by food shortages.

bly had its origins in or on the frontiers of China. Nine-tenths of the population of the northern province of Hebei are said to have died of the plague in 1331.

The government also maintained a competent fire brigade. In cities that were built mostly of wood and bamboo, lighted by candles, and heated by stoves, fire was an ever-present threat. In Hangzhou, for example, specially trained troops were stationed in raised sentry posts scattered throughout the town. At the first sign of flames, they would sound an alarm drum before rushing to the threatened buildings with ropes, ladders, scythes, and signal flags. Such groups could be more than 100 strong, and they operated with remarkable efficiency. But not all city dwellers trusted the fire brigades' ability. Prosperous citizens—perhaps bearing in mind the great blaze of June 1132, which destroyed 13,000 houses in Hangzhou—often paid to deposit their valuables in stone towers set within moats on the edge of the town. The moat offered protection against fire, while armed guards made the contents secure against theft.

Crime fighting was in the hands of civic magistrates, who acted as both detectives and prosecuting lawyers. They had their work cut out for them. In Changan, for example, members of flourishing youth gangs drew lots, using colored balls, to ascertain the identity of their next victim—red for a government official, black for a civic official. There were also secret societies, with evocative names like the Red Eyebrows and the Yellow Turbans, formed in order to achieve revolutionary political or messianic religious goals. One twelfth-century group believed that life was suffering; hence, the more people a devotee murdered, the more meritorious it was.

The bustle of Chinese cities was reported to the West by the Venetian traveler Marco Polo, who visited Hangzhou in the thirteenth century. Polo found the place overwhelming and judged that it was "without doubt the finest and most splendid city in the world." He described in awestruck tones the walls of the city (which he reckoned to be about ninety miles in circumference), the ten great markets (each 160 acres), the stone warehouses of the merchants, the immense variety of foodstuffs for sale, the bathhouses (unlike the Arabs, the Chinese preferred their baths cold), the streets reserved for prostitutes, astrologers, doctors, and other trades, the magistrates' offices, the organization of guilds, and the numerous canals that culminated in a boating lake on the south side of the city. The scale and number of everything was staggering, and it is no wonder that when Marco Polo returned to Europe and attempted to relate what he had seen, he was widely regarded as a liar.

Three centuries later, however, the West could no longer sustain its disbelief. By that time, Beijing had grown to be the largest city on the face of the earth, and a steady stream of travelers, missionaries, and merchants were reporting back on the wonders that they encountered.

But the awe would be short lived. For while Western civilization advanced, that of China remained in a state of static complacency. Secure in the cosmological certainty of their existence, Chinese emperors staunchly resisted any change. To them, China was the center of the world and the source of all civilization. And why not? The gap between the date of Chinese inventions and their eventual discovery by the West was staggering: 600 years in the case of letters of credit, 400 for movable type, 300 for gunpowder artillery, and an amazing 700 years for canal locks. Changan had had one million inhabitants in AD 700. Not until the nineteenth century would Europe's first city approach that size. But by then, China's civilization was already being overtaken by that of the industrialized West. When Britain's steam-powered gunboats arrived in China in 1840, they signaled a painful wrench into the modern world.

In the heat of a sixteenth-century July, Japanese townspeople *(left)* drag heavy floats through the streets of their capital, Kyōto, to celebrate the annual Festival of Gion. Founded in 794, the city was built on a grid plan in imitation of the Chinese capital of Changan. For more than a millennium, Kyōto remained Japan's capital, and although frequently devastated by warfare, flood, fire, and earthquake, it was rebuilt after each disaster along the same geomantically ordained lines.

REBIRTH IN THE WEST

"Why this excessive height, this enormous length, this unnecessary width, these sumptuous ornaments and curious paintings that draw the eyes and distract the attention from meditation?" Bernard, abbot of Clairvaux, was no admirer of contemporary architecture. "What ineptitude, and what expense!" he thundered in a letter to a fellow abbot. But Saint Bernard—he was to be canonized within twenty-five years of his death—was powerless to halt the wave of construction that was sweeping twelfth-century Europe. "A white mantle of churches," as one ecstatic monk put it, had descended upon the world.

Churches were only a part of the story. With a fervor rarely surpassed in Western history, men and women began to rebuild an urban culture that had languished since the Fall of Rome. New houses spilled out beyond the ancient walls of crowded towns. Castles sprang up in untamed lands, attracting frontier communities of settlers eager for space, adventure, and riches. And between these suddenly thriving towns and cities, people were on the move: pilgrims intent on glimpsing a fragment of the true Cross, Crusaders bound for the Holy Land, scholars, monks, beggars, and mountebanks. Above all, there were merchants, for the towns of western Europe were the children of trade. Spices from the Far East, wool from England, wax and furs from Russia, cloth from Flanders, wine from Burgundy—unceasing streams of mule trains spread across the face of the Continent. Where they stopped, at weekly markets or annual fairs, the cities grew in wealth and prestige, while within the city walls emerged a new class of independent citizen, determined to break free from the rule of bishop or baron.

It was by no means a golden age. Huddled beneath noble cathedrals were scenes of abysmal squalor; at times, thriving piazzas and marketplaces became stages for the barbaric justice practiced at the time. Power-hungry oligarchs crushed the democratic aspirations of their fellow citizens. Famine and disease routinely decimated the urban population. Nevertheless, the seed of regeneration had been sown, and it was in the urban landscape that it flourished. Here was distilled all the raw energy and imagination of a reawakened Europe. And here, culminating in the glories of the Italian Renaissance, were laid the foundations of modern commerce, politics, science, philosophy, and art.

City life did not collapse suddenly with the disintegration of the Western Roman Empire. The Germanic people who swept across continental Europe from the fifth to the seventh centuries AD stood in awe of the great civilization they had conquered and had no wish to see the cities they governed fall to ruin. But Europe's new rulers were totally unequipped to administer an empire of such size and sophistication. Inevitably, the cities decayed. In AD 537, water ceased to flow in Rome's Caracalla

Prosperous Florentines of the early sixteenth century gather at a street corner in this painting by Francesco Ubertini. One of the wealthiest European centers of the Middle Ages, with banking and trading interests stretching from England to Persia, Florence remained very much a family-oriented city. At the base of each house, a large, vaulted ground-floor room functioned as shop, warehouse, and workshop for the family occupants, while on the floors above, cooking, sleeping, and living quarters competed for space in unpartitioned rooms. As children were born and relatives arrived from the country, stories were added, creating a distinctive streetscape of tall, towerlike buildings.

Rising from the ruins of Roman occupation, the cities of medieval Europe stood as beacons of comfort amid a landscape ravaged by pestilence and invading tribes. At the city center, the church dominated a main market square, offering spiritual succor to the townspeople and traders who gathered there. The castle, meanwhile, threw its protective shadow over narrow streets that twisted and turned their way toward comfortingly massive city walls.

In addition to providing physical security, the walls acted as social frontiers. For medieval centers were breeding grounds for a new way of life. Here, merchants and artisans—the lifeblood of the city—congregated to escape the rigors of work on the land, and the concomitant subservience to a feudal overlord. When the city gates closed at dusk, they did so not only to protect the populace but also to safeguard the flowering of a new society.

The Bavarian city of Nuremberg *(below)* was one such seedbed. Founded in 1040, athwart the Pegnitz River, it boasted double walls, a deep moat, and numerous defensive towers. Trade, which flowed between northern Europe and the Alpine passes to the south, entered the city through five gates—one of which, protect-ed by a spiky police and customs barrier, can be seen in the left foreground. Within, cluttered streets of closely packed houses rose up to the central castle and church. By the late fifteenth century, when this engraving was executed, rising population numbers had forced many citizens to live outside the walls, as evidenced by the cluster of dwellings in the right foreground.

NUREMBERG: A WALLED SOCIETY

baths, designed to accommodate 1,600 bathers. Walls and aqueducts crumbled. Neglected temples and amphitheaters provided ready-dressed stone for simple dwellings or makeshift fortifications.

For a while at least, international trade across the Mediterranean Sea nourished a thriving cosmopolitan culture in ports such as Genoa and Marseilles. During the seventh and eighth centuries, however, this "Roman lake" fell under the control of an aggressive new power: the empire of Islam. In fewer than 100 years, Arab armies transformed the Mediterranean balance of power by means of a series of whirlwind conquests. Syria, Persia, the North African coast, and then Spain itself succumbed to this vigorous civilization, whose warriors were convinced their valor would win them a place in heaven.

No such assertive confidence sustained the people of Europe. Devout Christians withdrew instead to the security of monasteries, seeking in prayer and poverty, rather than acts of war, their souls' salvation. The monasteries, it is true, nurtured the seeds of learning throughout the centuries after Rome's collapse, but they did nothing to aid the political and economic recovery of a declining continent.

As international trade dwindled, the economy began to stagnate. A trickle of goods still reached the West by way of Constantinople, capital of Rome's surviving Eastern (Byzantine) Empire. Silks, drugs, spices, and jewels enriched the lives of a fortunate few, but the slaves, iron, and timber that Europe offered in exchange were of little value to the wealthy merchants of the East. For the ordinary person, life was a struggle to survive. Local markets within the gap-toothed walls of semideserted towns supplied those immediate wants—salt, cloth, or metal tools—that peasants could not produce themselves. Otherwise, they were rooted to their villages, laboring to sustain both themselves and the lord whose land they farmed.

In the absence of any overall, centralized control, society was held together by a pyramid of allegiances. The humble peasants owed their well-being to the local landowner on whose estate they lived and worked, providing labor in return for shelter and the right to grow crops for their own use. The landowners, for their part, maintained their position by acknowledging—with donations of military aid and a portion of their estates' produce—the overlordship of a more powerful neighbor. And that lord bowed in turn to a yet more distant and mighty baron. Wherever people existed, they did so only on payment of some due, in goods or labor, to the overlord within whose domain they lived.

Whatever political power existed was based on personal strength. And there was plenty of opportunity for Europe's powerful leaders to prove their mettle. For, impoverished and disunited, the Continent was easy game during the centuries following the collapse of Rome's empire. In their long swift ships, their hearts set on plunder, Viking warriors from Scandinavia brought terror to coastal and river settlements from Scotland to the Mediterranean. And near the end of the ninth century, with the Viking menace still at its height, Magyar hordes from central Asia swept into Germany and northern Italy.

It was a period of wretchedness and fear. Yet this dark age witnessed a development that was to reinvigorate the growth of cities and hasten the dawn of the medieval era. Demoralized by ruthless and unpredictable assaults, the embattled peasants and nobles of Europe rediscovered the ancient art of fortification. Together they strengthened the defenses of castles and monasteries, dug huge earthworks around unprotected settlements, and repaired the long-neglected walls of Roman towns. Into these strongholds they fled when pagan bands laid waste the countryside, and more often than not, their labors met with success.

The security of these fortified communities, or burgs, tempted an increasing number of refugees from the countryside to settle permanently within their walls. Some newcomers began to specialize in essential trades. Cobblers, saddlers, tailors, and bakers set up shop, freed at last from their dreary hand-to-mouth existence on the land. Other arrivals discovered a lucrative, if risky, new business in trade with nearby communities. For both merchants and craftsmen, the weekly town market was the key to prosperity. And with more goods to offer, the revitalized towns became magnets for the population of the surrounding area. Peasants began to rely on the town market for an increasing number of goods that they had formerly had to produce for themselves.

Trade attracted more trade. By the tenth century, the worst of the foreign invasions were over, but the towns continued to grow. A process that had begun in fear and self-defense was now a road to freedom and wealth. New communities blossomed outside the gates of castles and monasteries, while within the walls of former Roman cities, new houses sprang up on ancient foundations. The reborn towns were insignificant in comparison with those of neighboring civilizations. Many could claim only a few hundred inhabitants; an episcopal town, ruled over by a bishop, might boast a few thousand souls. In Britain, as late as the eleventh century, only a handful of centers had populations greater than 5,000. The Islamic cities of the Middle East, by contrast, were crowded centers of learning and commerce, while Constantinople had nearly one million inhabitants. As tiny as they were, however, the new European burgs contained all the ingredients of the urban revolution that was to ensue.

The watershed of the Continent's fortunes came during the eleventh century. One contemporary could even pinpoint the precise year that life began to improve: 1033, the millennium of the Crucifixion of Christ. It was then, according to Radulfus Glaber, a Burgundian monk, that God smiled upon the world once more. "The whole surface of the earth," he wrote, "was covered in pleasing verdure and in an abundance of fruits that put famine to flight." This was not pure fantasy. In fact, the climate had been gradually warming, a trend that continued for another 200 years. And while famine was by no means a thing of the

A friar doles out alms in this detail from a fifteenth-century French manuscript. Almshouses were set up in the fourteenth century to offer shelter to the poor, who had previously been housed with lunatics, pilgrims, orphans, and the sick.

A HOLY PROVIDER

The Church had remained isolated and insecure during the dark ages of barbarian invasion. Now, with the rebirth of European civilization, it emerged triumphant to dominate urban life. Gifts and legacies poured into Church coffers, donated by elderly penitents seeking a personal guarantee against damnation. Citizens contributed to their hoped-for salvation with land or labor according to their means. And as the fear of hellfire raged unabated throughout the Middle Ages, so the Church emerged as the largest urban property owner in Europe.

But the Church acted as more than a repository for sinners' silver. By the twelfth century, it had become a cohesive, continent-wide organization, directed from Rome, whose sphere of influence encompassed both the spiritual and physical well-being of its flock. At a time when temporal rulers were occupied primarily with gaining or safeguarding their wealth, it was the Church that administered the medieval social fabric. Church holidays were public holidays as well; both civil and criminal justice were administered by clerics; and virtually all education was provided by religious scholars.

Moreover, in canon law, the provision of charity was a moral obligation, and the Church shouldered the burden of this caring role. Using bequests and endowments, the Church constructed and maintained hospitals, almshouses, leper houses, orphanages, and hospices to shelter the weary traveler. The struggle of good against evil—as depicted on a crosier in the form of Saint Michael slaying the dragon (*above left*)—was unceasing.

Beds line the walls of Florence's San Matteo Hospital *(below)* in the early sixteenth century. Although intended mainly for the poor, Church-sponsored hospitals were open to all; the only prohibition was against wealthy patients' bringing their hawks and hunting dogs with them.

A marble relief from the tomb of a fourteenth-century Italian professor depicts law students at the ecclesiastical university of Bologna. Such academic subjects aside, the Church also organized training in embroidery, goldsmithing, and other manual trades.

past, improved agricultural methods—a better plow, for example, and more effective rotation of crops—ensured an increasingly reliable supply of food. Woodlands were cleared, and new land was brought under cultivation. The population burgeoned as men and women, released from fear and want, were successful in raising larger families to adulthood.

The revolution was more than agricultural. As the Muslim threat diminished around the Mediterranean Sea, there developed new opportunities for trade. The principal gateway to the East was Venice. This invulnerable city, strategically situated in the shallows of the Adriatic Sea, had maintained commercial links with Constantinople throughout the eighth and ninth centuries. Now other cities, chief among them Genoa and Pisa, reopened trading routes with the East. International trade expanded in the north, too, where Norsemen turned their seafaring skills to a peaceful purpose, opening up an east-west trade across the Baltic Sea. The high-quality, thick wool of English sheep, generally acknowledged as the best in Europe, also began arriving by the shipload at the ports of Flanders. The coastal towns of northern Europe, which had for centuries cowered in terror at the sight of strange sails on the horizon, now looked to the sea for their prosperity.

A new breed of people appeared in this safer, wealthier Europe. Plying their way along the Rhine River, or urging their mules over Alpine passes, long-distance merchants found an eager welcome in markets and fairs along their routes. Their dealings were simplified by the greater availability of money, for silver had recently been found in the Harz Mountains of Germany, and coins of small denominations gave people at all levels of society increased power to purchase the new goods that appeared in their market squares.

Money turned peasants into consumers. Money also turned them into townspeople. As feudal lords began to find it simpler to accept payment in cash rather than crops or labor, their tenants discovered that they were no longer wedded to the land. If the peasants had useful skills, they could earn money elsewhere, away from the drudgery and servitude of the estates. Many of them left the land for the growing cities and towns, where they could specialize in their trades and find a ready market for their goods. Farmers also appreciated the convenience of a center for selling their produce. Throughout the medieval era, town and country maintained a symbiotic relationship, each relying on the other for providing the necessities—and, increasingly, the luxuries—of life.

International trade, a money economy, more food, freedom from invasion—many factors contributed to the explosion of creative energy in the Middle Ages. A surge of building and commerce, of intellectual ferment and technological advances, typified the twelfth and thirteenth centuries. And the cities were where these dramatic developments transpired.

The evolution of the medieval city was not always peaceful, for it involved fundamental changes in the social order. The hopeful peasants and acquisitive merchants who converged on the walled towns of Europe were intent upon ridding themselves of their feudal obligations. They petitioned the bishop or prince who owned the town to grant them self-government, including the right to levy taxes, bear arms, promulgate their own laws, and coin their own money.

In order to obtain these freedoms, the merchants and artisans of many towns declared themselves members of a commune, bound by oath to defend their mutual interests. Reaction from their overlords was mixed. The Church was horrified at what it saw as a revolutionary and even heretical movement. "Commune! New and detestable name," protested Guibert, abbot of Nogent. "By it, people are freed from all bondage in return for a simple annual tax payment." The hostility of the Church to this new class of burgher arose partly out of traditional ecclesiastical opposition to any social change and partly from a belief that any profit in commercial transactions was akin to usury and was, therefore, a sin. The Church was to overcome the second scruple more easily than the first.

Nobles adopted a more flexible attitude toward the communes. Although some of them were antagonistic, many saw the benefits of renting their property for cash to the citizens of expanding towns, or collecting their tolls on the busy highways leading to the city market. Kings and princes, for their part, discovered that there was a political advantage to be gained from granting favors to an urban population that would subsequently side with them against rebellious nobles.

Throughout the twelfth and thirteenth centuries, the battle was fought and won. By force or by persuasion, cities and towns gained charters guaranteeing them freedom to govern their own activities. The terms varied. Some noble proprietors maintained a close supervision of their properties, still insisting on receiving every tenth pig, goat, or goose. Other cities, including many in Italy, had achieved virtual independence by the year 1200. Whatever the regional differences, one fact was universal: A new order of citizen had emerged, a "third estate" neither noble nor ecclesiastical—the bourgeoisie, or middle class. The free burghers enjoyed rights unimagined by their rural cousins. *"Die Stadtluft macht frei"*—"city air brings freedom"—boasted German burghers. Townspeople from Scotland to Sicily, in a hundred different tongues, expressed the same sentiment.

The power behind this successful revolution was the guild. At an early stage in city development, even before the advent of the commune, artisans and merchants had formed organizations to regulate business practices and maintain standards of production. Merchants' guilds jealously guarded the interests of city business leaders and sought to prevent the development of monopolies. Outsiders might be prohibited from owning a shop; basic foodstuffs could be bought wholesale only at specified times so as to eliminate unfair competition. Craft guilds developed high-minded standards of behavior and manufacture. Chandlers in the French city of Troyes were ordered to observe a weight ratio of sixteen to one for tallow to wick; butchers were not to sell the meat of dogs, cats, or horses. The spurriers of London were forbidden to work at night because of the nuisance to their neighbors and "by reason that no man may work so neatly by night as by day." Even the dice makers had a guild, which naively attempted to forbid the manufacture of loaded dice.

Guilds were not just commercial regulatory bodies. They were also social clubs, dramatic societies, and charitable institutions, and some had no craft function whatsoever. Guild members might be expected to dine together at regular intervals. They entertained the public with plays in the marketplace on holy days—lively elaborations on the Scriptures in which each guild staged an episode. When members fell ill, guilds helped support their families; they provided baptismal gifts and paid for funeral expenses. It was no wonder that the guilds also played a significant role in city politics. They petitioned, protested, and on occasion, they even led rebellions, forcing their noble proprietors to back down until all their demands were met. Guild leaders, particularly those from the wealthy merchants' guilds, were among the

Devils flee from the golden hand of God in a fifteenth-century miniature of Paris by Jean Fouquet, entitled *Descent of the Holy Ghost upon the Faithful.* During the reign of Philip II, from 1180 to 1223, Paris blossomed into the foremost city of northern Europe. Like many medieval centers, it was dominated by the Church—the Cathedral of Notre Dame, looming here against the skyline, was finally completed in the mid-fourteenth century after some 180 years' work. But it also bore the imprint of a powerful and civic-minded monarch: At Philip's command, the capital's 25,000 inhabitants were provided with new city walls, paved streets, and a sanitary water supply.

leading citizens of the towns and increasingly dominated the important political posts in city government.

A passionate sense of solidarity and civic pride inspired the burghers. "Let each help the other like a brother," advised a twelfth-century charter, and this is precisely what occurred. Indeed, the fraternal feeling even reached beyond the city walls. Several groups of cities formed leagues, promising peace, easing trade restrictions, and guaranteeing the safety of foreign merchants on their roads.

The cooperative movement reached its zenith with the emergence after the mid-twelfth century of the Hanseatic League, a commercial association of northern European cities, mostly on or near the Baltic and North seas. At its peak in the fifteenth century, the league comprised nearly 200 towns—chief among them Lübeck, Hamburg, and Bremen—from the Netherlands to the Gulf of Finland, and it had representatives in every major center from Russia to the Iberian Peninsula. When its interests were threatened, the league could go into battle with a navy the equal of any in Europe—and on occasion did so, with resounding success.

In the early days, however, the spirit of intercity unity was far from pervasive. Medieval Europe had weathered the dangers from without, but there was a constant threat of attack from neighboring cities or kingdoms, and fortifications were still first on any council's list of essential public works. It was not merely a matter of strengthening existing walls. The defenses that had sufficed in the eleventh century were no longer adequate for the expanding population 100 years later. New structures had to be built, encompassing the buildings that now lay vulnerable outside the town. Old walls were torn down, and their stones were reused for building. Sometimes, as in the Flemish town of Bruges, the course of an old wall's foundations served as a circular road within the expanded city.

Working on the town defenses was one of the several duties that a citizen had to perform for the commune. (Serving on the night watch and in the militia were other civic obligations.) Many of the walls were formidable structures, more than twenty feet high, and at least half as thick, pierced with tiny apertures through which unseen archers could fire a deadly rain of arrows. Leon Battista Alberti, whose fifteenth-century treatise on architecture covered every aspect of medieval town life, from designing piazzas to exterminating fleas, recommended building angular projections at intervals along the wall so as to catch an advancing enemy in a devastating cross fire. Rather more whimsically, he suggested facing the walls with massive, crudely dressed stones, "that the enemy at the bare sight of them may be struck with terror." There was little need for such psychological tactics. Until the advent of efficient siege artillery in the fifteenth century, stone city walls were a highly efficient means of defense. An enemy rarely succeeded in battering them down as long as there was adequate food and water within.

If the town walls were a labor of necessity, the cathedral was a labor of love. Christianity was a profound source of strength for medieval men and women, promising eternal salvation to people who knew only danger and uncertainty. Even during periods when famine and plague did not strike, an estimated 25 percent of the population would die before reaching the age of twenty. To build a cathedral was to create something as permanent as was within human power. It even transcended local politics; the members of a commune might be at war with their bishop while continuing to construct magnificent churches.

And there were times when it seemed that the enthusiasm for religious construction approached mass mania. "Men seemed to be born for no other employment but to build churches and chapels," the fifteenth-century architect Alberti would write later. Merely to participate in the physical toil of raising such edifices was seen by many as a way of acquiring heavenly favor. One Norman abbot was amazed to see wellborn men and women harnessed "after the fashion of brute beasts" to wagons full of building materials. "Sometimes a thousand men and women, or even more, are bound in the traces," he wrote to an English prior in 1145, "yet they go forward in such silence that no voice, no murmur is heard."

The greatest cathedrals and churches of Europe were erected with skill as well as with fervor, and their fine master craftsmen—masons, sculptors, glaziers, engineers, and carpenters—were internationally known. When Canterbury Cathedral in England was damaged by fire in 1174, it was a French master mason, William of Sens, who was hired to supervise the work of rebuilding. Such employment was well paid but was not without its dangers. When, in 1179, William fell from scaffolding high above the altar, the severity of his injuries compelled him to leave his task unfinished.

New architectural features replaced the sturdy, rounded arches of Roman tradition. The great engineering discovery of twelfth-century architects was that pointed arches, set at right angles to one another and supported by graceful flying buttresses from the outside walls, could soar to heights undreamed of a century earlier. Northern Europe adopted this new technique with characteristic passion. By the end of the thirteenth century, churches and cathedrals towered above the earthbound towns, monuments to the glory of God—and the ingenuity of man.

Not all public energy was expended on the Church. "This disease of building," as one twelfth-century bishop described it, infected the secular as well as the sacred aspects of city life in the Middle Ages. And as the era progressed, business affairs played an increasingly large role in shaping the city. Markets, the traditional centers of commercial activity, were at first in the open air; but as business increased, the markets were covered over and often enclosed by an arcade that included civic rooms above the ground floor for council meetings or official receptions. The wealthiest cities constructed grandiose market buildings. The thirteenth-century Cloth Hall at Ypres in Flanders, for instance, was a cathedral-like structure measuring 425 feet in length. The wealthy guilds, especially those of butchers and fish dealers, also celebrated their importance with impressive halls.

A fifteenth-century miniature records a commune of Flemish citizens receiving their city's charter. The granting of a charter by the baronial or ecclesiastical overlords of Europe's cities effectively transferred urban government to the hands of a commune, allowing medieval citizens to escape, to a large degree, the bonds and obligations of a feudal society. Some centers, the most notable of which were wealthy Italian towns such as Florence and Milan, became virtually independent city-states, refusing to swear allegiance to any overlord, engaging in their own foreign policy, forming leagues and alliances, and exercising almost total control over the surrounding countryside.

Nowhere was the mania for building more conspicuous than in Italy. There, the nobles, unlike the rural barons of northern Europe, removed themselves permanently to the cities, where they took to commerce with great enthusiasm. Because their rivalries frequently erupted into gang warfare, many of the nobles lived in heavily fortified compounds. Above these compounds, they erected tall watchtowers, upon which they occasionally placed catapults that they employed to hurl stones at one another. In 1177, Bologna had 194 such towers; and Florence, it was claimed, had 400 towers, one of them 250 feet tall. "Scarce a common housekeeper thought he could not be without his turret," complained Alberti, "by which means there arose a perfect grove of spires." By the fifteenth century, power was concentrated in the hands of a few families, rival towers were destroyed, and Italian cities assumed a less spectacular skyline.

Whatever their differences in outward appearance, medieval cities had certain elements in common. Chief among the buildings was the cathedral or principal church, usually situated near the central market square. Apart from its religious function, it was in frequent and varied use—as a forum for scholarly debate or a hall for civic banquets, or even as a covered market in early medieval days. Holy plays were staged there, processions began and ended there. Prosperous merchants, shopkeepers, and moneylenders established themselves around its walls, seeking the business and prestige that the cathedral would bring to their premises. Rents were accordingly high in the central area of the city, forcing poorer artisans to live and work on the outskirts.

The main square, often irregularly shaped, was flanked by the city's other principal buildings: the town hall and major guild hall, alongside an imposing inn or religious structure. It was hardly a solemn place, however. Only in a few tidy-minded cities, notably Florence, did the authorities seek to drive away the stall holders, hawkers, beggars, and idlers who were naturally drawn to this hub of excitement. Here was the stage for a startling variety of events—for public declarations of war and private business deals, for torture and executions, celebrations, bullfights, bearbaiting, and, where there was enough space, horse racing. The sacred and the secular, the noble and the cruel, were familiar companions in the medieval city.

While every large city had a center for social and political activity, there also evolved a number of self-contained districts, each with its own church, public fountain, and marketplace. Nowhere was this development more evident than in Venice, which had been constructed on a group of marshy islands. Even when bridges linked the islands, and the intervening waterways became the thoroughfares of a single great city, the sixty or so Venetian communities maintained their separate identities. They prayed to different saints, celebrated different festivals, and followed different local leaders. In spite of a dictatorial central administration, this patchwork of parishes in Venice and other major cities helped maintain a sense of solidarity and civic spirit among the medieval burghers.

A jumble of buildings caught in a crazy web of narrow streets, most medieval towns developed more from random accumulation than from any overall design. Where there was good transportation, a skilled work force, adequate security, and dependable sources of food and water, cities simply grew, with little or no forethought from civic authorities. Many important urban centers, including London, Florence, Cologne, and Milan, developed on the sites of former Roman settlements; but while some cities maintained at their core the regular crisscross of the ancient street plan, their medieval growth was a far cry from the monotonous grid of Roman towns.

Streets, although they often conformed to a roughly concentric pattern, frequently took surprising turns, their courses dictated by the hills, boulders, or streams that lay in their path. Alberti, writing at a time when broad, straight streets were in favor, acknowledged the advantages of an illogical town plan. Alberti put forth the argument that winding streets made a town seem larger. In addition, winding streets deflected winter gales, evenly distributed sunlight and shade, and ensured each house a different view. "Moreover," he wrote, "this winding of the streets will make the passenger at every step discover a new structure." Twists and turns even had a strategic value. Any invading army would almost certainly be stymied by the medieval maze of streets and alleyways.

Not all centers evolved so haphazardly. Inspired by the confidence and aggressiveness of their era, medieval rulers advanced into undeveloped, often hostile, territory, establishing new walled towns in frontier lands such as Gascony, Wales,

The emblem of the Florentine wool guild is shown here in an enameled terra-cotta relief by the fifteenth-century artist Luca Della Robbia. Guilds were of vital importance to the medieval urban economy, controlling the working conditions of most trades: hours, wages, employment, quality control, advertising, sales, prices, and the introduction of new technology. Nor did they restrict their activities to commerce: From the guild feasts they attended to the guild pall under which they were buried, members could expect their lives to be arranged with efficiency. So pervasive was the guilds' influence that even beggars, vagabonds, and thieves organized themselves along similar lines.

THE MERCHANTS' PROGRESS

A sculpture of a seagoing vessel, affixed to a house in mid-fifteenth-century Bourges, advertises the profession of its wealthy owner, Jacques Coeur. Coeur, who traded with the Middle East, was one of a growing number of international merchants.

The bond that united Europe's emergent civilization was commerce. Towns fed on trade, which in turn was encouraged by an ever-growing marketplace. And as merchants ventured farther afield, the Continent became crisscrossed with a network of trade routes that ran from city to city in a seemingly endless march of prosperity.

As populations expanded, so the small urban markets that had served the surrounding countryside became bustling entrepôts. By the late twelfth century, the French region of Champagne boasted six annual fairs, which drew an international clientele from all over Europe. It was not long before other centers followed suit.

As citizens grew rich, they sought to spend their newfound wealth and demand exploded for all kinds of goods. Each region learned to exploit its own specialty: Russia exported furs, wax, and amber; Bordeaux traded casks of wine; England shipped out bales of wool; salt for preserving fish and meat came from the Bay of Biscay; while barrels of herring and cod arrived from the countries of the North Sea. And as merchants discovered the riches of the Orient, a steady stream of spices and silks began to flow in from the Levant and beyond. Never, not even under the Roman Empire, had Europe witnessed commerce on such a scale.

A fifteenth-century Bolognese customer gets a fitting in an alley of drapers' stalls. As trade increased, such open-air enclaves became streets of more permanent structures with living quarters built over ground-floor shops.

Merchants in the textile center of Bruges sample a consignment of wine just unloaded by the port's crane. Powered by dual human treadmills and capable of pivoting on its base, the crane was one of many public amenities erected on Europe's docks.

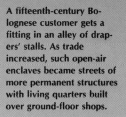

An English peddler shoulders his wares in this mid-fifteenth-century wooden adornment to a choir stall. Such itinerants were a common sight on medieval roads, carrying their meager bundles of goods to remote villages.

and Pomerania. Before his death in 1307, King Edward I of England authorized more than 100 such settlements in Britain and on the Continent, many of which were built by experts "who know best how to devise, order, and array a new town." Whatever their experience, however, such town planners were not encouraged to exercise much imagination. The streets of these fortified towns followed a rigid pattern, generally within rectangular walls. Typically, settlers would be given a long, narrow building site, of some 2,050 square feet, on which they would be expected to erect their own houses within a period of two years. Garden plots located immediately outside the town walls provided for their basic needs.

As trade and industry thrived, cities continued to expand, fed by a stream of hopeful immigrants. Peasants from the adjoining countryside constituted the rank and file of this incoming army, but many large centers attracted people from farther afield. Venice, one of Europe's most cosmopolitan cities, had important communities of Slavs, Greeks, Turks, Germans, and Jews. Indeed, so high was the death rate that without a constant influx of new citizens, urban populations would have dwindled. As it was, the medieval cities of Europe never achieved the size of their counterparts in the Middle East. (When European Crusaders sacked Constantinople in 1204, one Frenchman remarked in awe that more houses were destroyed by fire than there existed in any three cities in France.)

Italy, the chief beneficiary of Mediterranean trade, had by far the largest cities. The population of Venice in AD 1330 numbered about 120,000. Milan, its inland rival, was probably a little larger. (In 1288, according to one statistically minded monk, Milan had 6,000 public drinking fountains, 300 bakers, and 440 butchers.) Florence, Naples, Palermo, and Genoa were only slightly smaller.

North of the Alps, however, Paris alone could boast 100,000 citizens, while London and the great textile centers of the Low Countries—Ghent, Bruges, Ypres, and Douai—averaged perhaps half that number. Most other urban centers were tiny by comparison. Nine out of ten cities in northern Europe had fewer than 2,000 inhabitants. For the great majority of people, the only contact with urban civilization was through the myriad market towns that supplied the basic goods and services to neighboring villages. Even the important commercial town of Troyes in the Champagne district of France, where merchants from all over Europe converged for regular trade fairs, had a permanent population of no more than 10,000.

Medieval cities were a feast for the senses, although not every course was wholly welcome. They were crowded, noisy, dirty, bright with colors, and teeming with activity, much of it conducted in the open; they smelled like barnyards, or worse. Wheeled vehicles were still a rarity; in general, all but the wider streets were unpaved, and they were perpetually foul with mud and manure in the winter months. Some were mere alleys, in which two laden mules could scarcely squeeze past one another without knocking the goods off a shopkeeper's stall. Passersby had to watch their heads to avoid collision with awnings and the large signs that hung out over the street, advertising their services for the unlettered: perhaps a shoe fit for a giant, or a painfully realistic tooth announcing the services of a tooth extractor. Even the buildings—timber framed and three or four stories high—added to the sense of enclosure, their upper stories projecting over the lower ones and obscuring the light in the narrow space below.

Work was conducted for all to see. Shopkeepers would simply open the horizontal wooden shutters of their houses in the morning. The top halves became awnings; the bottom ones served as stalls for displaying their goods. The shopkeepers and their assistants worked in the rooms in the back, keeping a sharp eye out for likely customers. In many cities, an ordinance forbade shopkeepers to call out to customers in other shops, but the streets were far from quiet. There were sawing and hammering; clanging from the blacksmith; tapping from the coppersmith; creaking of signs; street cries from hawkers; curses from muleteers; squealing, barking, and honking (for medieval streets were full of scavenging animals); and the incessant ringing of bells from towers and steeples. Above it all was the intermittent bellow of the town crier, offering the full gamut of medieval news, from official decrees to births, deaths, and lost children.

Away from the city center, the din diminished. Here, the houses were meaner, often mere wooden shacks of one or two stories. In textile cities—and cloth was the making of many medieval towns—this was where the weavers lived and worked. Only the monotonous ticktack of the shuttle from a hundred household looms advertised the presence of this hidden work force.

At night, the streets fell silent and very dark, for there was no municipal lighting. In most cities, a curfew prohibited any outdoor activity after a certain hour. Otherwise, it was feared, poverty or political enmity would force people to commit desperate acts under cover of darkness. King William I of England insisted that fires and candles be extinguished at 8:00 p.m.—effectively forcing every English person into bed—and although most cities did not go to these extremes, only the night watch and citizens with special permits were authorized to wander abroad after the curfew. In Florence, a crime committed at night exacted a more severe penalty than the same offense committed during daylight.

An employee of the Siena commune receives his salary in the counting house of a fifteenth-century banker. The demands of thriving Italian merchants for easier access to capital led to the proliferation throughout northern Italy of private firms known as *banchi,* after the benches on which the moneychangers laid out their coins. They operated much like their modern counterparts: lending money, selling insurance, dealing in foreign exchange, and transferring funds by letters of credit. The larger banks, run by powerful families such as the Medicis and the Pittis, arranged credit and bills of exchange in cities throughout continental Europe.

These were violent times, and no cutthroat or rebellious mob acted with greater savagery than the law itself. Communal authorities did not take a more lenient view of crime than did bishops or princes. Castration, hanging, and amputations were commonplace. Severed heads routinely decorated the Tower of London, while quartered bodies fed the crows on the city's four principal gates. In Florence, a criminal would be dragged around the streets in a cart prior to public execution, his flesh torn with hot pincers. Once in a while, medieval law matched the punishment to the crime with macabre wit. An Englishman named John Russell, convicted of selling pigeons that were "putrid, rotten, stinking, and abominable to the human race," was pilloried, and his thirty-seven pigeons were incinerated at his feet, to the vast amusement of the onlookers.

While civilization was rising from the ashes in western Europe, Constantinople basked in the glories of a culture unsevered from its classical roots. As capital of the Byzantine Empire, it had been the beacon of Christian civilization throughout the Dark Ages. In the eleventh century, it reached its apogee as one of the world's richest, grandest, and most sophisticated cities.

To the medieval European traveler, the first glimpse of the metropolis was a formidable sight. Its imposing walls towered to heights of forty feet; while above them, on the city's seven hills, a profusion of roofs and domes soared to the crowning glory of the cathedral of Hagia Sophia, the heart of Eastern Orthodox Christianity.

Within the city gates, further wonders awaited the newcomer. Here were reservoirs, drains, and columned cisterns; the imperial palace, whose labyrinth of pavilions, chambers, and gardens was filled with mechanical marvels for the monarch's amusement; the Hippodrome, where chariot races drew crowds of as many as 60,000 people; and noble residences with ivory doors, mosaic floors, and costly rugs and furniture. Still more astonishing were the crowds that thronged the streets. At a time when the largest European towns numbered their citizens in the thousands, Constantinople was home to some one million inhabitants. In this city, visitors from the West might see more people in one day than they would in a lifetime at home.

Underlying this magnificence was a history of commercial success. Lying at the heart of the Mediterranean economy, the city had a perfect natural harbor and also stood guard over the great overland trade routes from the Levant, Kievan Russia, and the Far East. Constantinople was the marketplace of the world. Located in its streets of two-story colonnades were shops and workshops of every description: Here, one could buy furs, fine cloth, spices and medicinal drugs, precious stones and metals, while inside the shops, artisans turned raw materials into all manner of finery.

Behind the glittering facade undoubtedly lay squalor, but this could not diminish the city's glories. Its architecture influenced all nations who encountered it: The Basilica of the Holy Apostles, for example, shown below in a twelfth-century illumination, inspired Saint Mark's Cathedral in Venice.

In 1204, when plundering Crusaders sacked the city, much of its splendor went up in smoke. But it would be another two and one-half centuries before this glittering prize finally fell to the Turks of Asia Minor.

Fire was a constant hazard. Few ordinary houses were constructed of stone or brick. The spaces between their timberwork were filled in with wattle and daub—little more than twigs and plaster—while the roofing was made invariably from straw or reeds. Rows of such tinder-dry buildings would burn within minutes when a fire, ignited by a misplaced candle or a spark on the thatch, swept through the city streets. As a result, many councils issued regulations regarding the construction of buildings. After 1189, it was decreed, Londoners were required to build their houses of stone up to a certain height and roof them with slate or clay tiles. Disasters still occurred, however. In 1212, London Bridge, then crowded with shops and houses, caught fire at both ends. Three thousand bodies were fished out of the Thames River when the conflagration was over.

Teams of firefighters were organized in many large cities, but their buckets and carts were inadequate to combat the inferno that so often roared toward them. Their most effective technique was to tear down burning buildings with special fire hooks in an attempt to stop the blaze from spreading.

Fire had one beneficial result: It destroyed the verminous conditions that created serious health problems in every city. It was not that medieval people were personally unclean. Public baths were an institution that had survived since Roman days. In 1292, Paris had twenty-six such establishments distributed throughout its various quarters. Medieval Florence had three whole streets devoted to bathhouses. It was not until the fifteenth century that public baths became commonly associated with prostitution and fell into disrepute.

Nor were medieval people negligent of the sick or totally ignorant of contagious diseases. Hospitals were important institutions in every major city. Thirteenth-century Florence, with a population of nearly 100,000, had more than 1,000 beds for the sick. Funded by the Church and by private charity, hospitals provided a modicum of cleanliness and quiet for the patients—who often shared beds. These hospitals were frequently no more than almshouses or homes for elderly inmates. Many patients did not emerge alive from their stays, but at least they died in some decency.

But public baths and hospitals were not enough. As poor people continued to pour in from the countryside, medical knowledge and struggling city administrations were totally unable to cope with the resulting problems of sanitation, and by the fourteenth century, the disposal of human waste had reached a crisis point. Only the wealthy had private toilets and cesspits. Most of the population had to dump their ordure into open sewers or onto public dunghills. Even to hardened medieval noses, the stench was sometimes sickening.

City councils enacted strict laws regarding the disposal of waste. "We decree that no one shall throw water into the street, nor any steaming liquid, nor chaff, nor the refuse of grapes, nor human filth, nor bathwater, nor indeed any dirt," officials sternly cautioned the citizens of Avignon. Yet, in poorer districts, an alternative to the street did not exist; besides, lawmakers seldom had the resources to enforce their edicts. Some cities were worse than others. Siena, which had no drains, was particularly notorious. "The town not only stinks every night and morning when people throw their nastiness out of the windows, but even in the day, it is seen lying about the streets," observed a contemptuous Florentine.

No one enjoyed such sights and stenches, but the means to alleviate them were lacking. Paving was one technique that helped reduce the filth. Paris, in 1185, was the earliest city to surface its streets with stone. By 1339, all the streets of wealthy Florence were paved, but this was an exception; for the most part, side streets remained unpaved and unserved by sewers. Cleaning up the mess that had begun to accumulate in the medieval city was the work of many centuries.

Water supplies grew dangerously polluted. Early industrial effluent—particularly from the reeking tanneries—could be as noisome as its mid-twentieth-century equivalent. Water from the canals of Antwerp, it was said, killed even the horses that drank it. What was worse, wells and fountains grew polluted through seepage from cesspits and graveyards. Collecting rainwater or employing water carriers were two solutions; even better was bringing in pure water by pipe from outside the city.

Toiling workers pound cobblestones into position outside the walls of their city. By the time this fifteenth-century Flemish manuscript—possibly depicting Brussels—was executed, many European centers had given their muddy thoroughfares a hard surface. The first city to do so was Paris, where municipal funding provided for the paving of main streets in 1185. In the side alleys, however, where the reluctant inhabitants had to pay for their own improvements, the traveler still got dirty feet. Many cities also maintained roads throughout the surrounding countryside in the hope of attracting merchants—and their money—to the neighborhood.

This last method, however, had the disadvantage of rendering a city vulnerable to sabotage by besieging armies. London, which lived in less fear of attack than most European capitals, brought in water by conduit as early as 1236, "for the poor to drink and the rich to dress their meat." Although it was to be the ultimate solution, piped water was slow to gain general acceptance and did little to solve the immediate problems of disease.

Even more than human excrement and foul water, the greatest bane of European cities was the flea, specifically *Xenopsylla cheopis,* the pestilent parasite of the black rat. Plagues had swept through Europe before, but the flea-spread bubonic plague of 1348 to 1349, known since as the Black Death, was by far the worst that ever struck. "Many died daily or nightly in the public streets," wrote Giovanni Boccaccio, who witnessed the disaster in his hometown of Florence. "Of many others, who died at home, the departure was hardly observed by their neighbors, until the stench of their putrefying bodies carried the tidings." In all, one-third to one-half of the urban population of Europe died in less than two years' time. And bubonic plague continued to strike in the succeeding centuries. The population of France shortly before the Black Death had been about 21 million; in 1470, it was still only 14 million. City populations were kept artificially high by the continued influx of countrypeople. Even so, orchards, gardens, and vineyards now appeared within the city walls where the space to build a house had previously been unobtainable. Some believed the plague to be evidence of God's wrath; others diagnosed a release of noxious gases. The real culprits were never even suspected by medieval scientists. And as a result, *Xenopsylla cheopis* and its unsavory host continued to make themselves at home in the cities of Europe for centuries to come.

Disease, disorder, famine, and fire—the disasters that routinely turned life upside down—failed to dampen the burgher's capacity for enjoying city life. William Fitzstephen, an English monk, could find only two things wrong with twelfth-century London: drunkenness ("among the foolish sort") and the high risk of fire. Even the Black Death and subsequent plagues could not diminish the patriotism of Coluccio Salutati, chancellor of Florence in the late fourteenth century. "What city, not merely in Italy but in all the world," he wrote, "is more bedecked with churches, more beautiful in its architecture, more imposing in its gates, richer in piazzas, happier in its wide streets . . . ?'' The list continued.

All citizens loved the opportunity to dress up for a parade or a festival. "A city should not only be commodious and serious, but also merry and sportful," wrote Fitzstephen. There was ample opportunity for fun. Fourteenth-century Europe celebrated approximately fifty saints' days as public holidays each year. Processions typically involved representatives from the whole community winding through the city streets: Nobles and clergy, all the guilds from goldsmiths to cobblers, the night watch, shopkeepers, merchants—even a contingent of widows—participated. Carts lumbered over the cobblestones bearing familiar tableaux from the Bible: the Annunciation, Jonah and the whale, the three kings on their camels. Such formal observances were only part of a holiday. There were feasting and sports for all: Knights and nobles might joust or play tennis; for the ordinary burgher, there were wrestling, archery, soccer, animalbaiting, and even ice-skating—with runners made of bone strapped to the shoes.

And recreation was not confined entirely to one's own city, for medieval men and women had discovered the pleasures of travel. Apart from trade, the principal reason for embarking on a journey was to visit a shrine, cathedral, or other holy place. Frequently, the object of veneration was the relic of a saint or of Christ himself. The capture of Jerusalem by Crusaders in 1099 and the sack of Constantinople in 1204 had released a flood of "genuine" relics onto the medieval tourist circuit. There were two heads of John the Baptist, three crowns of thorns (in Paris alone), Christ's baby teeth, and several separate relics of his circumcision. Fragments of the true Cross abounded—enough "to make a full load for a good ship," the sixteenth-century Protestant reformer John Calvin irascibly observed. Such charlatanism was understandable if not justifiable. Pilgrims were a valuable source of revenue to a bishop hard pressed to complete a cathedral or abbey church.

And indeed, pilgrims had on occasion been the making of whole cities. The French town of Chartres, for example, whose church contained the sacred veil of the Virgin Mary, had grown up solely to cater to the relic seekers who arrived by the thousand. Rome, which boasted of being the "threshold of the Apostles," attracted as many as 50,000 pilgrims annually in the mid-fifteenth century. Equally prestigious as a place of pilgrimage was Saint James of Compostela (now Santiago), which claimed to be the final resting place of James the Apostle. Thousands of international pilgrims traveled the long road to this remote corner of northwest Spain, lining the pockets of landlords and shopkeepers along the way.

The explosion of building that occurred during the Middle Ages was not the only aspect of medieval urban development. A cultural and economic revolution was also under way. Learning, so long cloistered within the monasteries, was now more readily available through schools and higher institutions that were as often secular as religious. Italy had fourteen university towns by the fourteenth century, France had eight, and England two.

Society had grown increasingly complex. Aspiring lawyers were sent to study at a university—Bologna being the most highly regarded in this field—to reach the top of their profession. On a less academic scale, merchants, too, had to be literate and quick with figures, for commerce had become big business. Successful merchants no longer trudged from town to town, selling their goods for cash. They sat in their city

offices and supervised a team of accountants. They sent money by bills of exchange (guaranteed by one of the great banking houses in Florence or Genoa), insured their cargoes, and insisted on double-entry bookkeeping, which kept them up to date on their financial situation. The Italian peninsula was far more advanced than the rest of Europe in these commercial developments, and Florence—with thirty-three merchant banks in the fifteenth century—was the counting house of Italy. By 1345, some 10,000 young Florentines were learning to read, while more than 1,000 youths were studying arithmetic.

Prosperity and education stimulated curiosity. A wide range of inventions originated in the medieval era, from the striking clock to eyeglasses. People also began experimenting with gunpowder, a Chinese import that was to transform both the science of warfare and the nature of the city. But one area of study was to overshadow all others and result in a fundamental change in the way people regarded the world and their role in it. Strangely, it was an attempt to capture the past that led to the transformation of medieval culture.

Throughout the Middle Ages, scholars had marveled at the achievements of the Roman empire. It was not until the relatively tranquil and prosperous fourteenth century, however, that the study of antiquity made a significant impact on medieval life. While delving into the classical past—often through Muslim translations of ancient treatises—Italian scholars rediscovered an older world of philosophy, literature, and fine arts untouched by Christian tradition. Artists such as Giotto and

Michelangelo examined the medieval world with fresh eyes and created works of art that, though inspired by classical civilization, were no less products of their own time. Renaissance—or "rebirth"—this movement has been called. Its influence extended to the city as well.

More than any other nation, the Italians were inordinately proud of their cities. During the Renaissance, they began to see the possibilities of re-creating the architectural marvels that lay in ruins all around them. Architects studied the dimensions of surviving Roman buildings and pored over the work of Vitruvius, whose treatise on architecture, dating from the first century BC, was one of the key textbooks of the Renaissance.

Florentine officials, in particular, eagerly embraced the new ideas of Renaissance architects and town planners. The beauty of their city was an obsession with the Florentines. They welcomed opportunities for straightening and broadening the streets, opening up gracious vistas, clearing the piazzas of untidy shops, and erecting symmetrical palaces in place of the medieval buildings that leaned drunkenly over the pavement. Space and symmetry were the first two commandments of Renaissance town planning.

Private development was also altering the face of Renaissance Florence. The wealthy banking and merchant families, a self-styled aristocracy that essentially ruled the city, demanded houses constructed in the new classical style. Dozens of private palaces, portentous monuments to wealth and vanity, were raised throughout the fifteenth century. Some were individual works of art, but many were grossly at odds with their surroundings. Politically and aesthetically, the private palaces heralded the demise of the medieval city.

By the sixteenth century, a few privileged families had taken over civic administration, depriving ordinary citizens of any role in their destiny. City air no longer brought freedom. Indeed, the original pressing need to live in the city was fast diminishing, for city walls were no longer a guarantee of security. New artillery could shatter medieval fortifications. Powerless to defend themselves against besieging armies, cities surrendered their hard-won freedoms to larger political groupings. The age of the nation-state had arrived. Increasingly, power was concentrated in the nation's capital, a showpiece for ostentatious architecture and grandiose city plans. Medieval cities—the vigorous, independent communities that had transformed the fortunes of the Continent—had become victims of their own success. There was no place for them in the emerging states of modern Europe.

A winged lion, the traditional emblem of Saint Mark and the adopted symbol of Venice, recalls the saint's reputed interment there in 829. In the background of this painting by Vittore Carpaccio stands the Doge's Palace, from where the Venetian government controlled Europe's first maritime empire. After the sacking of the city's political and trading mentor, Constantinople, Venetian merchant ships dominated the seas, and colonies were established throughout the Adriatic and eastern Mediterranean. As one observer recorded in the late thirteenth century, "Merchandise passes through this noble city as water flows through fountains."

In *Tower of Babel*, the
sixteenth-century Flemish
artist Pieter Brueghel
the Elder denounces the
vainglorious quest for an
unattainable ideal.

"Earth has not anything to show more fair," declared the poet William Wordsworth on observing the panorama of London in the early nineteenth century. But for every such accolade to the glamour, glory, or energy of cities, there has been equal condemnation of their squalor, ugliness, and inhumanity. For centuries, artists and writers have acted as antennae of civic emotion, reaching above dry statistics to pick up citizens' own visions of their man-made environment.

As Western civilization emerged from the wreckage of the Roman Empire, so artists steadfastly portrayed the rosy ideals of their age. For medieval citizens, the heavenly city of Jerusalem—always shown as an implausible, glittering, European townscape—combined urban ambition with religious fervor. Later, the striving of Renaissance architects and town planners to re-create the ideals of classical antiquity was reflected on the canvases of the time: Orderly, serene streets stretched down lines of perfect perspective to capture a golden mean of proportion. Even when these imaginary vistas were replaced by less-fanciful panoramas in the seventeenth and eighteenth centuries, buildings were still shown at their immaculate best, the streets around them teeming with well-scrubbed, healthy poor.

With the advent of the Industrial Revolution, however, reality began to blister the veneer of idealism. Cities took on a life of their own, becoming self-propagating conglomerations that defied the boundaries imposed by any single creative vision. In the 1840s, the French poet Charles Baudelaire called for artists to represent "scenes of highlife and of the thousands of uprooted lives that haunt the underworld of a great city." It was not long before his cry was answered.

By the beginning of the twentieth century, the monolithic certainty of past ideals had been replaced by an acknowledgment of a city's diversity and of the emotions it could arouse in its inhabitants. London, the splendid capital city that had delighted Wordsworth in 1802, had taken on a different tone just a century later. In 1905, the author Ford Madox Ford described how, beneath "thunderclouds, the clouds of buildings, the clouds of corporations—there hurries still the great swarm of tiny men and women, each one hugging desperately his own soul, his own hopes, his own passions, his own individuality."

Both beauty and beast, the modern metropolis had become an entity built as much out of the hopes and fears of its inhabitants as of solid bricks and mortar.

Painted on a wooden chest around 1500, an imaginary Renaissance cityscape shows the geometric symmetry that was intended to

Painted in 1840 by Anglo-American artist Thomas Cole, _The Architect's Dream_ keeps the harsh reality of industry at bay with a melodramatic fan-

The haunted loneliness of city dwellers dominates the Norwegian artist Edvard Munch's depiction of an Oslo evening in 1891.

In an ominous vision of 1914, *Mystery and Melancholy of a Street* by Italian artist Giorgio De Chirico, a hoop-rolling girl runs a shadowy gantlet of threat.

In C. R. W. Nevinson's *The Soul of a Soulless City,* the dream becomes a nightmare. In this 1920 vista of New York City, a railroad carries the viewer into claustrophobic canyons of skyscrapers that have obliterated nature and have made human emotion invisible.

Buildings, bridges, and billboards overlap to create an image of urban restlessness, confidence, and diversity in Fernan Léger's 1919 interpretation entitled *The City.*

THE GRAND DESIGN

5 Early on the morning of Sunday, September 1, 1666, the lord mayor of London was warned of a blaze that had started in Pudding Lane near his house. He was not in the least worried: Fires, after all, were not uncommon in the huddled wooden buildings and narrow streets of the City of London, the capital's ancient heartland district. They were usually short-lived. "Pish!" he remarked, looking out of his window. "A woman might piss it out!" And went back to bed.

But this fire was different. It had been a hot August, and the town was tinder dry. A warm wind fanned the flames, which began to feed on the pitch-coated buildings, the timber sheds, the stacks of wood and coal on the wharves, and the hoards of tallow, oil, and spirits in the cellars. By Monday, the whole city was ablaze in a self-perpetuating firestorm, the rising hot air sucking in oxygen-rich cooler currents to feed the inferno. In the center of it all, the rotting pile of Saint Paul's Cathedral came crashing down amid a cascade of burning beams and molten lead.

There was only one remedy. On the order of King Charles II, sailors from the Royal Navy were brought in to blast firebreaks with gunpowder. By Tuesday night, the flames had subsided, leaving a wrecked, smoking city. By a miracle, no one was killed; but almost 400 acres were devastated, 88 churches lost, 13,000 houses destroyed, and 200,000 people made homeless. It was a catastrophe. But as King Charles realized, it was also a great opportunity.

The City had long been an unsanitary warren, a mass of narrow lanes, overhanging houses, and evil-smelling drains—a different world from the royal palaces and aristocratic houses upwind to the west, in Whitehall and Westminster. And oozing through it was the ordure-choked abomination, the Fleet River. Dramatist Ben Jonson painted a sickening picture of it on a hot summer's day, when the seat of every privy was "filled with buttock," and each stroke of the oars "belched forth an ayre as hot as the muster of all your night-tubs." The Thames River, into which the Fleet flowed, was merely a larger version of the same.

Since the beginning of the century, the population of London had doubled to 400,000, creating squalid slums that straggled down to the Thames. The death rate was high—smallpox and water pollution made London perhaps the most lethal place on the earth—but it made little difference. People continued to pour in from the countryside, pushed out by landowners enclosing common land for pasture and drawn by the concentration of wealth in the town. Plague was endemic, but even in the worst years—35,000 deaths in 1625, and 20,000 in 1665—it was never enough to slow immigration. The losses of 1625 were made good in two years. But for the fire, London would almost certainly have choked to death.

Now, here was a chance to plan a city properly, almost from scratch, with houses built of nonflammable stone, streets wide enough for traffic, and paving to combat the

An engraving of the mid-eighteenth century depicts wealthy Parisians promenading on the elm-lined Boulevard Saint-Antoine. Built over a section of Paris's old city wall in 1674, the boulevard typified the broad avenues that were constructed through Europe's cities from the sixteenth century onward, redefining cluttered medieval spaces with long, straight vistas. More than mere thoroughfares, however, the new streets also acted as social rendezvous where the rapidly expanding numbers of well-to-do gathered to see and be seen. Property developers cashed in on the popularity of these promenades, which came to form the centers of Europe's most fashionable urban districts.

KARLSRUHE: VISTAS FOR A KING

As power became concentrated in national governments, rulers sought to emphasize their might in the plans and structures of their capitals. Medieval cities had been dominated by their cathedrals; by the seventeenth century, they were centered on their seats of government—usually royal palaces. In capital after capital, the haphazard muddle of medieval streets was increasingly replaced by straight, central thoroughfares and streets lined with buildings whose uniform facades were modeled on the ideals of classical antiquity.

Karlsruhe, conceived in 1715 as the capital of the German principality of Baden, was one example. As depicted in this eighteenth-century engraving, the city was centered on the royal palace from which thirty-two streets radiated out into the surrounding town and carefully landscaped park. In addition to directing all eyes to the seat of power, the radial plan had defensive applications. As first devised by Italian military engineers, it allowed a centrally placed artillery battery to dominate every approach to the city.

accumulation of filth. Here was a chance, too, for Charles, newly installed on the throne after twenty years of republican rule, to create an enduring monument to the power of Restoration England.

Of several designs, the king chose one submitted by a thirty-three-year-old astronomy professor, Christopher Wren. Wren foresaw wide, straight streets leading to a new focal point: Saint Paul's, rebuilt in a domed Italian style that would rival Rome's magnificent Saint Peter's Basilica. After much dispute, construction began. It took thirty-five years—"slow as a Saint Paul's workman" became a catch phrase—but in the end, a masterpiece emerged.

Around it lay a remodeled London. Wren's farther-reaching plans were abandoned as too expensive, but the city was still a vast improvement over what it had been before the fire. Buildings were made of brick and stone. Except for the largest houses, which were limited to the main streets, dwellings were of four, three, or two stories, depending on the size of the street. And facades were flat and straight. Even the vile Fleet was dredged, cleaned, and reopened to navigation. During the half-century after the fire, London became sounder, safer, cleaner, easier to live in—a capital worthy of any nation.

London was not the only city to be transformed at this time into a living symbol of national power. Size was one indicator of this change: During the three centuries following 1500, Europe's population doubled to 200 million people, and the number of cities whose population was more than 100,000 increased from four to seventeen. London, the most extreme example of urban growth, increased its numbers more than seventeenfold to 865,000. But even more important was the qualitative nature of the change. The haphazard and often opportunistic rise of medieval towns was replaced by a deliberate, planned expansion. Settlements that had barely scraped by as cities during the Middle Ages became national centers of power that represented all the wealth and ambition of their people. Their rapidly expanding boundaries contained mighty palaces, grandiose civic offices, imposing monuments, and sweeping vistas surrounded by carefully designed streets of uniform facades—the lavish display of power that arose from increasingly centralized and wealthy governments.

For much of their inspiration, the rulers and designers of these new cities looked to the past. Since the fourteenth century, the urban dwellers of Renaissance Italy had been enjoying the benefits of a resurgent interest in classical learning. Scholars, architects, and artists worked hand in hand with wealthy patrons to bring the glories of Greek and Roman town planning—broad streets, open squares, and graceful, symmetrical facades—to their prosperous cities. Now, that pattern was being replicated throughout the Continent. As nations grew wealthier and more powerful, it was seen as only fitting that the style that had graced such mighty cities as Rome and Athens should now grace those all over Europe.

Nor was it in appearance alone that the great centers of Europe resembled those of classical times. For society was beginning to flourish and diversify in a manner unparalleled since the demise of Rome. As nations grew wealthier, the seeds of a mercantile middle class, sown in the Middle Ages, began to bear fruit. And the opportunities for commercial gain that the big city offered were matched by those for enjoyment. Whereas medieval life had often been a struggle simply to survive, now people had both the time and the money to relax. As the demands of the leisured rich spawned an increasing variety of urban entertainment, Europeans came out to play.

Perhaps more than anything else, this new vitality exemplified the latest innovation in urban development. The era of the capital city had arrived.

Many different factors combined to reshape the old medieval towns of Europe, with their tightly huddled houses that were constrained by thick defensive walls. From about 1500, Europe's agriculture had enjoyed a slow but steady improvement, as increased land clearance, intensive cultivation, and more efficient land use produced a surplus of food. The threat of large-scale famine, which had dogged life in the Middle Ages, was steadily receding. At the same time, European merchants were beginning to turn away from the safe, tightly controlled trade routes of the Mediterranean region toward the unknown, wider world. Sailors from Spain and Portugal, then those of the Netherlands, France, and England, made Europe the master of the globe, discovering and dominating the Americas, coastal Africa, much of India, and the Far East. Gold and silver plundered from South America, spices from the Orient, slaves from Africa—these and countless other new trade goods undermined the traditional dominance of Mediterranean ports, swinging the balance of economic control northward.

Related to these two elements were a spate of technological and cultural innovations: the development of gunpowder, which made ancient defenses obsolete; the advent of printing, which eased the flow of information; a passion for new knowledge, reflected in an increasing number of universities and academic institutions; and the introduction of new banking techniques. The changes fed on one another and increased the people's demand for services that were available only in cities.

One of the first areas to witness the combination of all these factors was the Netherlands. Since the fifteenth century, increased land reclamation by drainage had produced the food to sustain a larger population. And the region's coastal ports were well placed to exploit Europe's trade, channeling southward the grain, furs, and timber from the Baltic region, and receiving, in turn, spices, wine, and salt from the Mediterranean.

Business-minded Amsterdamers throng their city's new stock exchange in a 1668 painting by Job Berckheyde. Stocks and shares had been negotiable in Europe since the fourteenth century, but in Amsterdam, the Continent's commercial center during the seventeenth century, the volume of dealing reached unparalleled proportions. Speculators came from as far away as Moscow, Persia, Turkey, and India to gamble on the price of virtually anything—from tulip bulbs to shares in the Dutch East India Company—and fortunes could be made from a judicious piece of inside knowledge. One gambler boasted that he could make "100,000 crowns in a day . . . if he learned of the death of the King of Spain five or six hours before it became public news."

No port grew fatter on its profits than Amsterdam. In 1550, the city's population was 30,000; it doubled by 1600, doubled again by the mid-1620s, and again fifty years later. "There belongs to this town a thousand ships," wrote an awed English visitor in 1586. The city's flag—three white crosses on a black and red background—was known in every port in Europe. And it was not long before Dutch seafarers began exploring the possibilities of trade farther afield. In 1602, the Dutch East India Company, one-half of whose sixteen directors were Amsterdamers, was set up. The company, which by 1650 had 15,000 vessels—60 percent of the entire European fleet—became the most powerful trading entity in the world.

Of equal importance to Amsterdam's growth was its spirit of tolerance during a time of fanaticism. After the northern Netherlands declared their independence from Spain in 1579, Amsterdam emerged as the dominant city of a loose federation known as the United Provinces. The official religion was Calvinism, but the provinces' 16,000 Catholics were allowed freedom of worship. A seventeenth-century Amsterdam minister wrote with pride that "you may be what the devil you will there, so you be but peaceable." This tolerant atmosphere paid dividends. Refugees flooded in from more oppressed areas, such as Spain, Portugal, and France, bringing with them their skills and capital.

As more goods and more people arrived in Amsterdam, the place began to burst at the seams. A new city was needed, one that would provide housing, reflect Amsterdam's growing wealth and, at the same time, improve trading facilities. A mud flat at the mouth of the sluggish Amstel River was not the best site for an expanding city—one Englishman called it the "great bog of Europe." But beneath the mud lay solid ground. Buildings could be secured on piles and the water controlled by canals. By 1609, the city council, which ran every important aspect of town life with remarkable unanimity, had purchased about 1,300 acres outside the old medieval walls, approved a plan for development, and ordered construction to start. Over the next fifty years, they supervised the building of three great half-moon canals leading from the main harbor, each navigable by barge and bisected by some 600 minor waterways. The plan was a telling indictment of the inadequate size of the old town: The innermost canal followed the course of the city's ancient medieval moat.

The council strictly controlled building on the resulting islets, which were sold to private developers on the open market. Successful buyers had to construct their houses out of the material ordained by the council, usually brick; had to install a privy for each dwelling; and had to pay for the maintenance of the footpaths and canal banks that ran past their property. Zoning ordinances set aside harbor frontages for warehouses, main canals for merchants' mansions, and side canals for the homes and businesses of artisans and craftsmen. But whatever the zone, Amsterdam betrayed its origins as a child of commerce. Even in residential areas, the houses were built at a forward pitch of as much as five degrees, allowing the unhindered passage of goods—hauled via a sturdy hoist set into the gable—to upper floors that were invariably reserved for commercial storage. As competition for waterfront space intensified, Amsterdam grew into a city of tall, narrow buildings, through whose large windows sunlight percolated into the gloom of deep interiors.

At the very heart of the city, meanwhile, stood the twin symbols of Amsterdam's

Captured in 1607 by the brush of Aegidius Saedler, members of the public browse through traders' stalls in the Vladislav Hall of Prague's Hradčany Castle. Although they were seats of national power, Europe's royal courts were far from closed to their subjects. Until the end of the eighteenth century, many of them doubled as fashionable shopping galleries. This castle area in Prague, for example, contained booksellers, print shops, haberdashers, and even toyshops.

SQUARES OF DISTINCTION

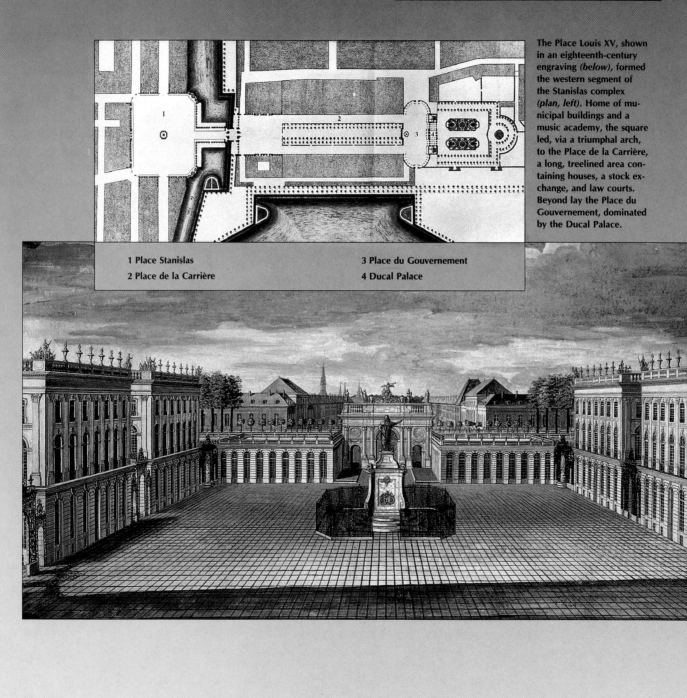

The Place Louis XV, shown in an eighteenth-century engraving *(below)*, formed the western segment of the Stanislas complex *(plan, left)*. Home of municipal buildings and a music academy, the square led, via a triumphal arch, to the Place de la Carrière, a long, treelined area containing houses, a stock exchange, and law courts. Beyond lay the Place du Gouvernement, dominated by the Ducal Palace.

1 Place Stanislas

2 Place de la Carrière

3 Place du Gouvernement

4 Ducal Palace

In the lively jumble of medieval cities, shops and houses, poor people and rich clustered together in the same quarter. By the early seventeenth century, however, a new concept in city planning had appeared—the residential square. It might be square, oval, or triangular and consist of a leafy garden or a cobblestone space for carriages; the houses around it, though, displayed ranks of elegantly uniform facades, signs of the distinction of their wealthy inhabitants, who lived well separated from their poorer neighbors.

The first such square was the widely imitated Place Royale in Paris, completed in 1612, but the idea reached its most graceful and varied realization in the French town of Nancy, when the Place Stanislas was created for Stanisław Leszczyński, exiled king of Poland and duke of Lorraine. Here, architect Héré de Corny built from scratch a series of independent squares and fused them into a sweeping plan that was an architectural summary of all that the modern city might need: royal and private residences, an academy, a stock exchange, law courts, a town hall, billiard rooms, cafés, shops, and a leafy promenade. Construction started in 1753, and just two years later, Nancy was adorned by a harmonious masterpiece of architecture, greenery, and water that formed the administrative, commercial, social, and residential center of the town.

might: the town hall and the exchange bank. Completed in 1655 on a foundation of 13,659 sturdy, Scandinavian-pine piles, the town hall was grander than any existing palace in Europe. Behind its stone-clad, classical facade, the council ran the city in a setting of soaring columns, rich marble floors, tapestried walls, and valuable paintings. Meanwhile, the exchange bank, founded in 1609, provided the means whereby businesspeople could make payments by credit transfer without using coins. Soon, merchants, governments, kings, and politicians from all over Europe were using the service. All recognized the efficiency, confidentiality, security, and reliability of the city's banking system. By the end of the seventeenth century, more than 16 million Dutch florins were lying on deposit in the bank's capacious vaults. Amsterdam had become the financial capital of the Western world.

Amsterdam may have been one of the wealthiest cities in Europe, but by 1700, it was no longer the largest or the fastest growing. First place was by then shared by two cities, Paris and London. In addition to the impetus of their expanding populations, each of these towns was at the hub of something totally new in European history: a centralized nation-state.

Although many of the cultural and political elements of nationhood had already existed for more than a thousand years, Europe had been divided into great estates—duchies, kingdoms, and princedoms by the hundred—whose owners acknowledged higher allegiances only when forced to do so. Sovereignty over large areas depended on ephemeral alliances with local rulers and the ability to assert dynastic claims. Sometimes the areas welded together by overlords coincided with present-day national frontiers; but often, particularly in Germany and Italy, they did not.

Paradoxically, France emerged as a united nation only from the jaws of disintegration. During the second half of the sixteenth century, while the Netherlands was prospering on foreign trade, France was riven by internal discord. In 1562, the civil war that broke out between Catholics and Protestants heralded more than thirty years of intermittent strife. And no part of the country suffered more than Paris. The city and the king were frequently at odds, even though both were Catholic: To Parisians, the court seemed to concentrate on war and pleasure, turning to the city only for taxes or troops. In 1588, the Parisians deposed their monarch, the lackluster Henry III, and blockaded the city against him.

Paris sank into squalor. The water pipes were broken, the wells were contaminated, and the garbage-ridden streets—the first to be paved in Europe, and once the pride of the Continent—became so full of holes that horses broke their legs when they stumbled in them. Housing was appalling: There had been virtually no worthwhile residential or royal construction in the city for two centuries. What dwellings of substance there were merely served to underline the divisions within Parisian society. The residences of the rich were built like fortresses and were supplied directly from their owners' country estates. In times of trouble, the better-off would often simply flee to the country.

It was Henry's successor, the Protestant Henry IV, who broke the deadlock, with remarkable simplicity. "Paris," he declared, "is well worth a mass," and in 1593, he became a Catholic. The following year, he was allowed to enter the city, proceeding to the cathedral where he knelt, symbolically paying the price for his capital. Meanwhile, his supporters ran through the streets promising amnesty for all.

With peace came revival. During the preceding three decades of religious conflict, politicians had increasingly seen the need for some kind of central control, formulating their theories into the concept of a sovereign's divine right to rule. The monarchy, it was stated, had been created by God and was responsible only to God. All French people, whatever their faith, must therefore obey the king, for to do otherwise would be in direct opposition to the Almighty. It was a sweeping mandate to rule, and one that Henry exercised with both tact and gusto.

While continuously reminding Parisians of the dangers of civil strife, Henry imposed his will with care, taking control of the police, courts, and prisons. In pursuit of his vision of Paris as an obedient, peaceful, and prosperous city, he appeared frequently in public, flattering, listening to complaints, and speaking with obvious sincerity of the "public interest."

Paris visibly benefited. In 1599, Henry ordered his chief councilor, Maxmilien de Béthune, duc de Sully, to supervise the construction of new, wider roads, bridges, open spaces, and buildings. In 1600, by a new royal decree, unsightly sheds were torn down, carpenters were forbidden to block roads with their lumber supplies, and tanners were banned from drying their products in public. "All carters carrying and conveying manure and materials emptied from privies, mud, and other filth are forbidden to unload elsewhere than in ditches and gutters designated for this purpose," ran one edict. "And also, all persons are forbidden to throw any water, filth, or garbage from the windows . . . under penalty of two crowns' fine and prison." In all this, Henry maintained a close personal interest, always with an eye to good public relations. Just before the completion of the city's new bridge, the Pont Neuf—which, at ninety feet wide, was not only broader than any European bridge but also any existing city street—the king visited the site. He saw how close the two unfinished

Flemish skaters cavort on the ice at a carnival held outside Antwerp's massive walls in about 1600. With the advent of siege artillery, city fortifications were built on a vast scale, but the open spaces in front of them—necessary for a clear field of fire—became popular gathering places; and their broad ramparts attracted promenading citizens in search of fresh air. Those at Antwerp, designed by an Italian military engineer, were beautified with a triple row of trees. And as improved military technology rendered them obsolete, the fortifications remained oases of space in an expanding city.

ends were and leaped the gap between them, to the delight of the assembled workers.

In brief, Henry's brand of what was later to be known as enlightened despotism laid the foundations of the modern city of Paris. Unlike most of his nobles, Henry possessed no country chateaus, and he refused to waste the country's wealth on any grand cathedrals. Instead, in the words of one of his subordinates, he was "motivated by a just desire to do good for everyone, to provide work, and to increase the incomes of the common people."

To this end, he commissioned a series of galleries, 1,970 feet long, between the Louvre palace and the Tuileries gardens. Galleries were in fashion as showcases for works of art and for banquets, but no one had seen anything as huge as this. Henry had a personal interest—the structure provided him a back way out of the city in case of trouble—but he was also acting altruistically. He installed artists and craftspeople in the space created, the arts—as he wrote—"having greatly flourished as a result of the peace, and being of very great convenience to the public."

Henry was no expert, but he knew what he liked: grand vistas and commanding monuments, preferably in the classical styles of Renaissance Italy (his wife was the daughter of Francesco de Medici, duke of Tuscany). Upon learning of new buildings being built in a particular street, he reminded Sully, "It would be a fine ornament to see this street with a uniform facade."

Two examples of the king's influence were the Place Dauphine and the Place Royale. The most important building project since the construction of the city walls in the thirteenth century, the Place Dauphine transformed low, uneven, muddy ground near the Pont Neuf into a triangle of elegant, Italianate four-story residences, trimmed with golden Seine-Valley limestone and topped with high slate roofs. Such a geometrical arrangement, totally new north of the Alps, affected all Parisian design from then on. The Place Royale, later renamed the Place des Vosges, was equally effective. Moreover, with the vital stimulus of royal sponsorship, both projects were financed out of the private funds of wealthy citizens.

The king also made provision for the sick. Previously, medical care—often simply almshouses for the elderly and crippled—had been in the hands of monasteries and other religious institutions. At the best of times, they were overstrained: During epidemics and droughts—there were about 5,000 to 10,000 plague victims every summer—peasants would pour in from the surrounding countryside in search of relief. But during the civil wars, Paris's rudimentary medical services had collapsed altogether. In a burst of activity, Henry founded two new hospitals, one of which, the Hôpital Saint-Louis, was specially reserved for plague and leprosy victims.

By the time of Henry's death in 1610, at the hands of a fanatic assassin, Paris was reborn. The city's population had taken a century to double, growing to 220,000 by 1600, but the next doubling took place in fifty years. The capital was increasingly seen as the center of the nation, and the wealthy flocked to be at this hub of power and influence. Aristocrats, royal officials, judges, and successful merchants all owned country homes. But for nine months of the year, they were absentee landlords, preferring to live in their grand townhouses, or *hôtels*. And with them came the wealth from their great estates, which poured into the capital to finance building projects and to provide employment. A growing number of domestic servants and shopkeepers—grocers, haberdashers, goldsmiths, furriers, and hatters—acted as an accurate index to the influx of cash.

Not all, however, profited from the new prosperity: Paris was still sharply divided

The burgeoning wealth of Europe's nation-states was reflected not only in the grandeur of their cities but also in the increasingly leisured lives of their inhabitants. Medieval amusements—short-lived fairs and occasional parades or contests—had occurred wherever the space could be found for them. Now, more permanent venues, such as those shown here and overleaf, were developed to satisfy the needs of a pleasure-hungry society. From theaters and operas to assembly rooms and coffee-houses, these buildings and the areas surrounding them became intimately interwoven with the new urban fabric.

Frequently, the structures had a sporting theme. Tennis courts, which were available to rich and poor alike, proliferated throughout Paris during the seventeenth century—although these were often later converted into theaters. Viewing stands were erected so that the less energetic aristocrats could watch races or—in Spain and Portugal—bullfights. And the amateur sports enthusiasts, or Corinthians as they were known in England, of all classes were attracted by the flying blood and feathers of the cockpits.

In addition to the sporting venues, there were many places where people went simply to meet one another. Coffeehouses provided a congenial atmosphere for business discussions and gossip. The open vistas of Europe's new boulevards were popular areas for socializing; in London, specially designed pleasure gardens, complete with or-

SOCIETY AT LEISURE

chestras, restaurants, and wine bars, beckoned. Theaters, too, were as much public assembly rooms as playhouses. During any performance, the floor might be thronged with gentry strolling, glass in hand, between groups of their friends. And off season, the theaters were used for balls and the newly popular masked entertainments known as masquerades.

Throughout all of these social encounters ran the thrill of sexual intrigue, for the meeting places frequently served as marriage markets. Apparently, not everybody got a good bargain. The English novelist Daniel Defoe recorded the outrage of British matrons, who feared that the events merely encouraged "half-pay officers to run away with their daughters."

The new approach to leisure reached its zenith in Europe's spa towns, such as Bath in Britain and the original Spa in eastern Belgium, sought out for their mineral springs. Favored at first for the medicinal quality of their waters, they rapidly became social centers where people came not only to cure ailments but also to dine, gamble, and dance. The combination of informal gaiety and rural charm proved irresistible to both society and real estate speculators. In Bath, for example, the master of ceremonies worked with a quarry owner and two architects to create a beautiful city devoted to pleasure—a place in which the increasing numbers of wealthy Europeans could pursue a new way of life. The result was the world's first planned resort.

An etched fan shows the fashionably ill congregating to take the waters at Bath's Pump Room in about 1737. A typical daily regimen at the spa included two visits to the Pump Room, where the indisposed met to gossip, drink three glasses of warm mineral water, and listen to music.

A convivial couple enjoys the fare at a Dresden coffeehouse in 1770. Coffee—just one item on an extensive menu—was often served in elaborate porcelain pots, such as the one shown below, which was made in the nearby Meissen workshops.

Operagoers take in a show at Rome's Teatro Argentina in 1747. Built five years earlier, the vast, tiered auditorium was often packed to overflowing: Seats were not numbered, and spectators simply squeezed in until there was no more room.

between rich and poor. The *hôtels*—complexes of courtyards, stables, gardens, and storehouses—were self-contained worlds, presenting blank walls as if the streets themselves were the enemy. Outside swarmed the mass of poor Parisians, *le peuple*. A fortunate few earned reasonable wages in the city's luxury enterprises—glass and wallpaper factories, and a few porcelain and pottery works—but most inhabitants scraped by from the money they earned as cheap labor or from selling goods made in workshops situated within their own rented accommodations.

In time, the economic disparity would lead to revolution and bloodshed, but during the first half of the seventeenth century, the position of the French monarchy was increasingly consolidated. Under the iron regency of two successive chief ministers, Cardinal Armand Jean Richelieu and Cardinal Jules Mazarin, the French court began to wield unprecedented power. Richelieu had promised to make the king the "most powerful monarch in the world." By the time of Mazarin's death in 1661, such power seemed almost within reach.

The king concerned was Louis XIV, who assumed personal power upon the death of Mazarin, who had been principal minister during Louis's minority. An apt pupil, Louis knew, with God-given certainty, that order, prosperity, and power were indissoluble. "I am the state," he said, meaning he either was, or would become, the fount of all authority, morality, and taste, the very epitome of absolutism.

Louis's preferences had two dramatic consequences for Paris. First, because he abhorred the teeming, odorous multitudes, he built his own court to the west—upwind from his stinking subjects—at Versailles. As a result, construction toward the eastern part of the city virtually stopped, and Paris reached out obsequiously westward, with the vast mansions, gardens, and stables of status-hungry aristocrats creeping toward the new court.

Second, Louis was determined to bring order and discipline to his unruly capital and to make it subservient to his authority. This task was undertaken for him by his chief minister, Jean-Baptiste Colbert, a sober-minded draper's son who took it upon himself to knock sense into all of France's body politic. Industry, commerce, taxation, the navy, the arts, and the colonies would all be made to serve the greater glory of France and its monarch. And Paris, as Louis wished, would become the capital of the greatest empire since ancient Rome: "It is certain," Colbert wrote, "that it sets in motion the rest of the kingdom."

The adherence to the Roman imperial ideal demanded the creation of buildings in obedience to the classical rules of proportion and solidity, with deep foundations, perfect stone, iron bars to reinforce arches, and lead chinking. That was the way, so Louis thought, to make buildings immortal and to ensure the immortality of the sovereign to whom they were dedicated.

It was a vision Colbert pursued with obsessive zeal. His architects examined old buildings to discover the sources of the best stone. To decorate his monuments, he ordered Roman iconography—tombs, inscriptions, arches—to be copied exactly. When Louis withdrew to Versailles, losing interest in his plans for the capital, Colbert pressed on alone, commissioning streets, piers, markets, and fountains. Manufacturing and commercial enterprise were restricted to specially demarcated areas. Squatters were cleared, artisans were fined for blocking traffic with their wares, and building codes were enforced. The old city walls, no longer needed for defense, were replaced by broad treelined walks. Where their gates had stood, there now rose monumental Roman arches. Great hospitals—Salpétrière and Hôtel des Invalides—

were constructed, each evoking the same imposing and somber monumentality.

The remodeling of Paris involved more than just a face-lift. Colbert's schemes also extended to the control of everyday life. He took a passionate interest in every detail of city management—street cleaning, hygiene, firefighting, riots, epidemics, building standards—and appointed a lieutenant general of police, Nicolas La Reynie, who shared his vision. La Reynie's department, with its 48 investigators and some 2,500 assistants, assumed a wide range of responsibilities. Besides investigating crimes and making arrests, they maintained a comprehensive network of spies, monitored prisoners, and censored seditious and pornographic novels.

One particular area of police interest was the city's growing number of cafés, or coffeehouses. Introduced from the Ottoman Empire, coffee drinking had long been a popular pastime in London. But it was not until 1675, when a Sicilian, Francesco Procopio, set up a *maison de café* complete with chandeliers and marble tables, that cafés became fashionable in Paris. Here, high society met to partake of coffee, lemonade, chocolate, confectionery, and Italian ices, as well as to hear—in the absence of independent newspapers—semiprofessional news tellers known as *nouvellistes*. And amid all of this lurked La Reynie's spies, disguised as kitchen staff or customers, ears cocked for subversive gossip.

The spy-filled cafés were just one example of the Parisians' growing desire to enjoy themselves. While existence in the medieval city had been work and church centered, with fairs and religious holidays forming the only entertainment, well-off city dwellers were now beginning to turn to leisure as a way of life. As the court grew more prestigious and wealthy, and as more and more of the aristocracy gathered in the capital, so "society" demanded entertainment. They found the spacious vistas of new Paris ideally suited to their needs.

In 1616, Henry IV's Italian wife had laid out the Cours la Reine, a triple avenue of elms running alongside the Seine River. It was to this and similar venues that society

A 1747 engraving by William Hogarth portrays a popular amusement for London's poorer classes—a day out in the fresh air at Tyburn gallows. Hanging days were declared public holidays, on the reasoning that the sight would act as a deterrent to crime. But the thousands who thronged the fields around Tyburn, the city's principal place of public execution, found the experience exhilarating, if not positively restorative. Spectators would cheer the condemned before pressing forward to touch the corpse, which they believed possessed healing qualities. At the end of the day at a nearby alehouse, souvenir hunters could purchase sections of the rope, at six cents per inch, from the hangman.

A cartoon by Thomas Rowlandson, entitled *Miseries of London*, lampoons the teeming humanity who, despite improved street planning, made travel in London a nightmare at the beginning of the nineteenth century. Besides running a gantlet of horse-drawn carts, coaches, and carriages, pedestrians had to sidestep mud-choked gutters, dodge lumps of excrement hurled from windows above, and duck under shop signs—such as the one shown on the left of the picture—which frequently fell down to maim passersby. A further danger came from sedan chairs, the conveyances of the wealthy, whose bearers enjoyed running their poles into the backs of slow-moving or unwary foot travelers.

flocked in their finest outfits and most glittering coaches, to show off, meet, gossip, conduct affairs, find spouses, and get the latest news. The central avenue of the Cours had room for six coaches to drive abreast, and on a normal day, it was packed with as many as 800 flamboyant, aristocratic conveyances. It was a showcase for the city's finest, where everyone came to see and be seen. The Marquis de Rouillac, who presented a pair of gloves to every lady who took his fancy, was an example of the former; the Sieur de Molins, who once drove the length of the Cours with his bottom sticking through the window of his carriage, an instance of the latter. When the king came out, the numbers swelled even further, bringing the whole procession to a standstill for hours on end. The royal presence—consisting, in 1662, of seven coaches, each pulled by eight horses—was literally a show-stopper.

By 1715, the year of Louis's death, the elegant Parisian style of living had become a model for the elites of other European countries. As the century progressed, open spaces in cities throughout the Continent were transformed into neatly designed areas for social gathering. In London's Pall Mall, the well-to-do played the popular Italian ball game of *pallamaglio;* in Berlin, high society paraded under the lush trees of Unter den Linden; wealthy gondola-borne Venetians glided in musical processions along the Grand Canal; Amsterdamers strolled along the alleys of the newly drained Nieuwe Plantage district.

Europe's rulers also took their cue from the Paris of Louis XIV and his successors. From the Elector of Saxony to the emperors of Prussia and Austria, all, it seemed, were determined to remodel their capitals as shining examples of their absolute power. But none went about the procedure as deliberately as Czar Peter the Great of Russia. A brilliant, wild, and intensely curious autocrat, Peter was determined to force his backward country into the modern world. The creation of a new capital, built from scratch and planned according to the current vogue for orderly and imposing classical styles, seemed the perfect means of demonstrating his success to the West.

The site chosen by Peter was a small island at the mouth of the Neva River, wrested from Sweden in 1703 to provide an outlet to the Baltic Sea. There, on May 27 of that year, Peter laid the first stone of a new fortress, thus marking the foundation of Saint Petersburg, present-day Leningrad. Thousands of conscripted Russian laborers toiled under the direction of imported French and Italian architects to turn their czar's dream into reality. Foundations were sunk, ornate palaces were planned, and broad, straight streets were laid out. By 1712, Peter's vision had taken concrete enough shape for him to move the Russian court from Moscow to Saint Petersburg and declare the city his new capital.

Every aspect of Saint Petersburg owed its existence to the czar's commands—even the city's population. A long series of decrees provided for the forcible settlement in Saint Petersburg of both artisans and nobles. It was a deeply unpopular move: The place was marshy, fogbound, constantly flooded, and unhealthy. Of 1,000 carpenters drafted by a decree of 1713, more than one-half had run away within a year. Nevertheless, population numbers steadily grew. Commerce, too, was pressed upon the city. From 1713, a series of orders demanded that Russian products such as tar, potash, and caviar be exported only through Saint Petersburg. By 1726, the new capital accounted for 90 percent of the nation's foreign trade. The very material from which the new capital was built was a result of Peter's ordinances. As there was no stone in the region, a new tax was introduced: Every wagon entering the city had to bring at least three stones, every boat ten, and every large ship thirty.

When Peter died in 1725, Saint Petersburg was still in a state of muddy disarray. But the basic plan was there, and construction continued apace—avenues, war offices, palaces, academies, ministries, cathedrals, and aristocratic mansions. And throughout the rest of the century, Russia's new capital continued to grow, spreading its imposing granite embankments along the Neva, and throwing out bridges to link more and more islands. By 1800, the "Venice of the North," as it became known, housed a population of 220,000 and was the acknowledged cultural, educational, and social center of the Russian Empire.

Even while rulers such as Peter the Great were modeling their capitals on Paris, the dominance of their shining absolutist example was being challenged. For by 1700, London had taken over as Europe's fastest-growing and richest capital, and the world's leading commercial center.

Like Paris, London was the seat of a powerful government and the acknowledged hub of the nation to which the landed gentry flocked with all the wealth from their estates. But there the similarity stopped. Unlike its continental counterparts, London was not home to an absolute, all-powerful ruler. The period of republicanism preceding Charles II's Restoration had left the country with a representative parliament whose power far outweighed that of an increasingly constitutional monarchy. Great Britain—as the nation was called following the union in 1707 of England and Wales with Scotland—was the nearest thing in Europe to a democracy, and the individual liberty that its people now enjoyed was reflected in an ever more enterprise oriented culture. London, by the eighteenth century, was a city of opportunity—and by the 1760s, the largest industrial center in Europe—whose myriad businesses catered to the needs of an increasingly affluent population.

Equally critical to London's expansion was its increasing significance as a port. For Britain was a growing commercial power, and onto the docks of its capital poured all the commodities from far-flung colonies and trading partners: furs, tobacco, and cotton from the Americas; sugar from the West Indies; textiles from India; spices from Indonesia and the Malay Peninsula; fish from Newfoundland; and tea from China. In addition, there was a regular flow of goods to and from the Continent, and cargoes of corn, coal, meat, timber, and other essentials arrived daily from the provinces to support the burgeoning city.

So great was London's shipborne trade that more than one-fourth of the city's inhabitants worked on the waterfront. And there were plenty of willing hands looking for employment. In just one generation, the population had increased by almost 50 percent, from 400,000 at the time of the fire to approximately 575,000 by 1700; another 300,000 would be added over the next century. This growth was largely the result of immigration, which more than made up for a hideously high death rate. The majority of these newcomers were from the surrounding countryside, but many came from farther afield. There were Portuguese and German Jews, French Huguenots, colonies of Irish families, parishes of abandoned black slaves and, around the docks, houses packed with ship-jumping Chinese deck hands and discharged sailors from the East Indies. One eighteenth-century survey found that only one-fourth of all Londoners were born there.

Not all newcomers found the capital's accommodations to their liking. Rents in Wren's new houses were beyond the means of the majority, and the poor were forced to live out on the capital's fringes in artisan dwellings that were often jerry-built slums. All new buildings had to be made of brick, but the lines of uniform terraces were constructed only to make a quick profit. Few houses were expected to last beyond the sixty-one or ninety-nine years of their leases, and they often collapsed before then. London, wrote lexicographer Samuel Johnson in 1738, was a "place where falling houses thunder on your head."

Nevertheless, urban life was, on the whole, getting better. From the early eighteenth century, a plethora of Improvement Acts were passed to ameliorate conditions in the city. Under the aegis of the various commissioners detailed to effect these improvements, the face of London began to change. Fine, flat stones replaced the round pebbles that had formerly been used for paving; unprotected open cellars and coal chutes were covered; stalls, billboards, and balconies were removed to let in light and air; houses were equipped with downspouts to channel rainwater from roofs into new gutters that ran along the side of every street; and even if trash was still dumped in the middle of the road, at least there was now provision for its collection.

Every district chipped in with its own regulations. Some met with more success than others. In 1716, for example, the City of London decided that individual homeowners should hang out their own lamps to light the streets—from 6:00 p.m. to 11:00 p.m. on the winter nights when the moon was at its dimmest. The cost-conscious citizens declined to accept the invitation, however, and that part of London remained sunk in a pall of darkness. It was several decades before taxes were raised to provide public street lighting, and the gloom was dispelled. Even then, the result was not overly sophisticated—small tin vessels, half-filled with cheap oil or fish blubber, sputtered within dirty glass globes—but, at a time when cities such as Paris were still poorly illuminated by candles and flaming torches, London at night was the marvel of Europe. When the prince of Monaco visited the city in the 1780s, he believed the streets to have been splendidly illuminated in honor of his visit.

Efficient street lighting was just one example of the way in which centralized control was tightening its grip on London. By the latter decades of the century, most public services were provided by taxation. But many of the improvements owed their existence to private patronage (and an eye to a profit) rather than to the single monolithic vision that had dictated the growth of Paris and Saint Petersburg.

The west of the city, as always, was the preserve of the aristocracy, now eagerly investing in property development on their estates. One such was Lord Burlington, who, in the early eighteenth century, leased land to those willing to adopt the Italianate pillars and porticoes of his favorite style, one developed by Andrea Palladio more than a century earlier. Palladio's writings had been translated in 1715, and he was widely copied in England, as in the rest of Europe, by those with pretensions to architectural elegance.

The fashion caught on. Throughout the eighteenth century, architects such as Robert Smirke, John Nash, Henry Holland, Nicholas Hawksmoor, and Robert Adam toiled under the direction of their aristocratic patrons to create squares, streets, and churches, all modeled on the glories of classical times. Even the lowly slum builders found it easy to follow the uniform lines of Palladian proportions—though stripped of all extraneous ornament—and directed their ephemeral attentions accordingly.

Growth and development made for a pulsing, exuberant street life. Whole streets turned into shopping centers, catering to the needs of an increasingly consumer-

Mexico City's Plaza de la Constitución mirrors the grandeur of imperial Spain in a seventeenth-century painting by Cristobal de Villalpando. According to the Law of the Indies, laid down in 1573 by Philip II of Spain, Spanish colonial settlements were built on a grid plan centered around a market square. Strict control was exercised over the location of streets, churches, monasteries, and industry. The plaza, whose sides were more than 900 feet long, was the biggest square in Latin America and contained all the features laid down by imperial edict, including shopping arcades *(right of picture)*, a main church or cathedral *(left)*, and a building for the royal council or viceroy *(center)*.

oriented society. Fashionable covered arcades were built to provide a comfortable spending environment for wealthy patrons and their attendants—and, in the case of Lord Burlington, to provide a barrier against the oyster shells thrown over his mansion wall by mollusk-eating idlers. Outside on the streets, vendors hawked their wares, trying to attract the attention of less-moneyed customers. Meanwhile, the thoroughfares were thronged with pedestrians dodging the rattletrap hackneys that creaked shakily over the cobbles. In addition to these hired conveyances, there were some 5,000 private coaches, many of them six-horse contraptions followed by a train of luggage carts and pack animals. These wrestled for space with sedan chairs, brewers' drays, butchers' wagons, and dung carts. The congestion was no less along the waterfront, where travelers were accosted by watermen with a cry that disconcerted newcomers: "Oars! Will you have any oars?"

There were endless amusements for the visitor to Britain's capital. Down by the Tower of London stood the royal menagerie, housing lions, tigers, leopards, and a dog with two legs. In the museum of the Royal Society, those of an inquiring bent could gaze upon the latest scientific discoveries of the time, as well as such curiosities as a "piece of bone voided with his urine by Sir William Throgmorton." The death-row inmates of Newgate Prison were a popular attraction. Just a few pennies would buy an entertaining visit to "Bedlam," the Bethlehem Hospital lunatic asylum. And for those with more money to burn, London was the widely acknowledged gambling den of the world. Bets could be placed on virtually anything, from games of chance to dogfights and political contests. Gentlemen's clubs made book on wagers such as the age at which their members would die or the number of children their wives might have. One wealthy politician, Charles James Fox, gambled nonstop for twenty-four hours, losing money at the rate of £10 a minute. There were thousands like him.

A less expensive time could be had in one of the city's many new pleasure gardens. Here, all classes of society from royalty to clerks gathered to hear orchestras, drink punch, attend fancy-dress balls, and meet lovers beneath the treelined walks. Alternatively, Londoners could amuse themselves at one of the many fairs and freak shows that had become permanent features of the city. Wonders such as "Tall Saxon Women" and "Corsican Fairies" drew crowds—as did, according to one advertisement in 1778, an "Ethiopian Savage" plus a "very remarkable foreign Cat, and an extraordinary exploit done by a wild mouse."

Other diversions became ways of life. Chocolate and coffeehouses were so popular that, by the early years of the century, there were more than 500 of them, many catering to specialized interests. At Will's, one could chat with men of letters; lawyers were to be found at Nando's, artists at Old Slaughter's, marine insurers at Lloyd's, soldiers at the Little Devil, and whores at Tom King's. A London merchant habitually spent an hour every morning at such an establishment, rarely starting his six-hour working day before 10:00 a.m.

But while London enjoyed all the benefits of a freewheeling and increasingly capitalistic society, it also endured its drawbacks. The strict control exercised by La Reynie's Paris police was not to be found in Britain's capital. Instead, Londoners preferred to rely on bands of night watchmen, or "thief takers"—urban bounty hunters who were paid per felon delivered to justice—and small groups of law-enforcement officers who operated under the supervision of local magistrates.

Despite the best efforts of this uneasy coalition, crime remained a serious problem. Even in the most refined surroundings, there were pockets of villainy (Thievery Lane in Westminster was well named), and members of the aristocracy themselves were not beyond reproach. Gangs of young dandies, such as the Mohocks, Nickers, and Bold Bucks roamed the streets torturing night watchmen and prostitutes. Especially worrisome were the frequent interracial riots that erupted within the city's diverse population. For, despite a remarkable lack of color prejudice, Londoners were notoriously contemptuous of foreigners (who were collectively despised as "French") and nourished a particular hatred for the Irish, whose Hibernian lifestyles—and competitive wages—were deemed disgustingly low.

In times of grave crisis, the army might be called out to deal with unrest. But even then, the authorities were loath to disrupt the natural course of events. During the signally vicious Gordon riots of 1780, which ended only after some 850 deaths, the lord mayor of London querulously dithered at the head of his troops: "I must be cautious what I do lest I bring the mob to my own house." For all its vigor, London was far from being the utopia that its classical facades might suggest.

By the time London roared and bustled its way into the nineteenth century, numerous other European cities had embarked upon rapid, self-sustaining growth. Municipal planning and the health of the population had improved to such an extent that most cities were now growing as a result of natural increase as well as immigration. London, with suburbs expanding in every direction, was well on its way to becoming Europe's first city of one million people. And even the depredations of the French Revolution in 1789 failed to stop Paris's expansion. Saint Petersburg was prospering, and two other imperial capitals—Berlin and Vienna—had grown rapidly under autocratic eighteenth-century rulers. Each displayed its standing with eye-catching displays of authority: In Berlin, capital of the expanding Prussian state, the Brandenburg Gate rose as a triumphal symbol of Prussian military might; and Vienna boasted the power of the Austrian empire at Schönbrunn Castle, its own version of Versailles.

The growth phenomenon was echoed overseas. From the viceroyalties of Spanish America to the provinces of British India, colonial capitals developed into administrative and trade centers modeled on those of the mother country. Even in the United States, which had only recently thrown off its colonial status, the European pattern was adopted. In 1800, the American government moved to Washington, D.C., a new, specially built city, geometrically designed in the classical style by a French-born architect, Pierre L'Enfant.

By the dawn of the nineteenth century, the world was dominated by throbbing, vibrant capitals, each carefully designed to make manifest its position as a national center of power. It remained to be seen, however, if their carefully planned streets and classical facades could survive the challenges of the future. For one among their midst carried the seeds of a new force that would threaten the established patterns of authority. Already, by the late eighteenth century, British entrepreneurs had discovered the commercial benefits of steam power and the factory system; and their nation's capital was not deaf to the sound of money. Cash was now king. And as the sooty fingers of industry reached out to clasp first London, and then cities around the globe, urban life began to move to a new rhythm. In the years to come, industrialization would bring growth of a size and speed unforeseen in dream or nightmare.

URBAN OASES

Amid the artificial landscape of the modern city, open spaces such as New York's Central Park *(below)* stand as civic lifelines to nature. But for centuries of European and Asian history, such havens were restricted to the private grounds of kings and nobles. Commoners might occasionally be allowed into these verdant oases of aristocratic privacy, but on the whole, they took the air wherever they could find it—in once-private orchards rendered ownerless by plague, along the broad ramparts of for-

tified cities, or under the leafy avenues of a monarch's newly designed capital.

As cities expanded and prospered, however, they began to engulf the outlying gardens and hunting grounds of the nobility. By the eighteenth century, it had become impossible to deny the public at least limited access to these spaces. At the same time, the creation of parks became positively prestigious, as landowners sought to imitate the "natural" vistas created in Britain by landscapers such as Humphrey Repton and Lancelot "Capability" Brown. The city of Munich acquired a public *Englischer Garten* in the 1790s, and in the years to follow, the English ideal—serpentine lakes, along with carriageways and footpaths curving sinuously through gently sloping, folly-dotted woodland—was re-created throughout the Western world.

By the mid-nineteenth century, the park had become a vital part of urban planning. The moral and physical benefits to be gained from fresh air, exercise, and contact with nature were, in the view of social reformers, as necessary to citizens' health as clean streets and efficient sewers. And if the industrial city's grimy expansion into the surrounding countryside could not be stopped, it could at least be mitigated by the creation of green spaces that provided recreational facilities for all. No longer an outpost of privilege, the park had become part of the civic patrimony.

PRIVATE PARKS AND PLEASURE GARDENS

The aristocratic stranglehold on fresh air was broken first in London. Beginning in 1637, in steady succession, the royal parks—Saint James's Park, Green Park, Hyde Park, and Kensington Gardens—were opened to the public until, by the 1790s, Londoners could stroll amid a wide, green belt that stretched for almost two miles through their city.

Not all such change was peaceful. In France the revolutions of 1789 and 1848 turned large swathes of Parisian green space into national property. And many of the gardens of Japan's ruling shoguns were not opened to the public until after their owners were overthrown in 1868.

Other open areas owed their origins to commerce rather than conflict. The gardens at Vauxhall, Ranelagh, and Cremorne were an important part of London's nightlife in the eighteenth and nineteenth centuries. In these amusement parks, visitors paid to dance, promenade, eat, drink, and watch entertainment such as fireworks displays or balloon ascents. The fashion quickly spread to the Continent, and by the nineteenth century, most European capitals boasted pleasure gardens.

Worshipers at Tokyo's Kan'eiji Temple admire the cherry blossoms around Shinobazu Pond. This view was painted some fifteen years before the grounds were opened to the public in 1873 as Ueno Park.

High society, led by the Prince of Wales, parades in Saint James's Park in the mid-eighteenth century. London's royal parks retained much of their exclusivity long after they had been handed over to the public.

Pleasure seekers gather like moths around the bright lights of Cremorne Gardens. In 1877, after thirty-five years of profitable business, the gardens were closed because of complaints from longsuffering local residents.

PLAYGROUNDS FOR THE PUBLIC

As the pall of industry settled on the globe, so the public park became an integral part of civic life, planned from scratch on land specifically laid aside for the purpose. The first such was Liverpool's Birkenhead Park, designed in 1843 by Joseph Paxton. Others soon followed. In 1850, Paris had less than fifty acres of municipal parkland; twenty years later, following the city's reconstruction by Baron Georges-Eugène Haussmann, that figure had risen to nearly 4,500 acres. And in 1896, American architect Frederick Law Olmsted—creator of New York City's Central Park—strung a ring of interconnected parks like an "emerald necklace" around the expanding city of Boston.

As parks proliferated, so their function diversified. Areas that had previously been aristocratic enclaves for socializing, strolling, and an occasional duel now offered all manner of amusement for every class of citizen: boating lakes, bandstands, and botanical collections; teahouses, tennis courts, and zoos. As Olmsted wrote of Birkenhead, "The poorest British peasant is as free to enjoy it in all its parts as the British queen." The park had come of age.

A children's camel ride passes the bustling refreshment area of Berlin's Tiergarten in this lithograph of 1880. Opened in 1844, the Tiergarten had the world's first public zoo.

The streets and avenues of a remodeled Paris reach out to incorporate the former royal forests of the Bois de Boulogne *(far left)* and the Bois de Vincennes *(left)* in this 1873 plan.

Fashionable young Parisiennes of 1900 show off their "rational" cycling costumes in the Bois de Boulogne. Mature trees up to sixty feet high were planted to give the Bois a landscaped, English look.

THE AGE OF METROPOLIS

Something astonishing was happening to the Scottish town of Glasgow. In the early eighteenth century, when the writer Daniel Defoe described it as "one of the cleanliest, most beautiful, and best-built cities in Great Britain," about 14,000 people lived there. By 1780, it had an impressive 42,000 inhabitants; still, as a local historian observed, "every stranger is charmed with the appearance of Glasgow; the streets are clean and well paved"; most of its stone houses were "in exceedingly good taste."

But by 1818, when its population had tripled once more, the charm had vanished. In the wake of the city's first recorded typhus epidemic, an alarmed investigator described the "hovels which the poorest classes inhabit" as "depositories of wretchedness." And things were getting worse. In 1839, when the city's population stood at almost 250,000, an appalled member of a government commission reported what he had seen during an official survey: "I did not believe, until I visited the wynds of Glasgow, that so large an amount of filth, crime, misery, and disease existed in one spot in any civilized country." By the end of the 1840s, another 70,000 people had crammed themselves into the municipal boundaries, regardless of the typhus and the cholera that ravaged them. It was the price of progress. For the clean little town on the Clyde River had become something altogether new: an industrial city.

During the nineteenth century, the urban order that had prevailed throughout the Western world was turned dramatically on its head. Ever since European civilization had dragged itself from the confusion of the Middle Ages, the increasing wealth of nations had been concentrated in prosperous capital cities, seats of power whose ordered streets and vistas, embellished with graceful, uniform facades, were designed to reflect all the glory of classical Greece and Rome. The hammer of industry rudely shattered that serene vision. Power was now wielded by machines rather than by monarchs. And no stately concept of town planning could cope with the massive impact of industry and its accompanying work force. Moreover, industry sprang up wherever its resources were available, and regional centers now vied with the capital for national importance. Glasgow, for example, had not just grown in size: By the middle of the century, it was one of the most dynamic centers in Great Britain, with opportunities and wage levels that were almost the equal of anything in London.

And Glasgow was not alone. Other British centers, too—Birmingham and Manchester (approaching Glasgow's size), Leeds and Cardiff, Liverpool and Belfast—were growing, unplanned and seemingly of their own volition. Although none approached London in proportions—in 1841, the capital's population was more than two million and rising—their expansion was of a magnitude that both impressed and appalled contemporaries. As an English newspaper declared in 1832, in mixed tones of satisfaction and alarm, the "manufacturing system as it exists in Great Britain, and

With the onset of darkness, Chicago, capital of the Midwest, presents a dazzling panorama of arrow-straight streets and soaring towers. Founded in the early nineteenth century on the swampy shores of Lake Michigan, the city grew rich processing the grain, timber, and livestock of the surrounding prairie. Faced with the problem of streets that were almost permanently covered with mud, the town council came up with a drastic solution in 1856: It raised the whole city—roads, sidewalks, and buildings—more than three feet above ground level. In the 1880s, Chicago gave birth to an even more impressive phenomenon—the skyscraper. The urge to build up soon spread, and the high-rise office complex was established as the unmistakable symbol of urban America.

BIRMINGHAM: A VISION OF ENTERPRISE

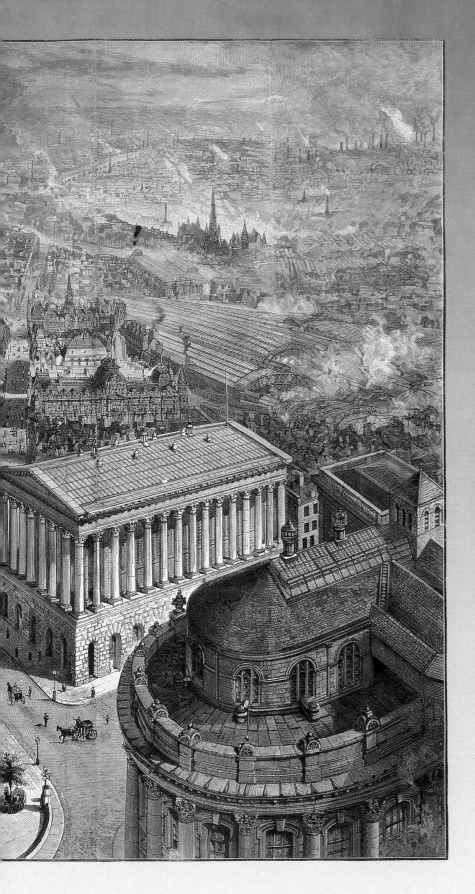

In the nineteenth century, the impetus of the Industrial Revolution transformed Britain's provincial towns into clamorous cities dedicated to the production and distribution of machine-made goods on an ever-increasing scale. The effects were most conspicuous in those towns that had grown up beside rivers—whose power now drove the machines and whose waters became highways for the transportation of the finished products—and were soon apparent across Europe and the United States.

The ugliness of the new urban conglomerations was condemned by writers such as Charles Dickens: In his 1854 novel *Hard Times*, the city of Coketown is made up of "vast piles of buildings full of windows where there was a rattling and trembling all day long, and where the piston of the steam engine worked monotonously up and down, like the head of an elephant in a state of melancholy madness." But in many cities, the wealth generated by the new machines fostered confidence and civic pride, and in the city centers, there arose a panorama of grand public buildings.

In this bird's-eye view of Birmingham in the English Midlands dated 1886, for instance, the main square is surrounded by educational institutions that include an art gallery, a museum, and a library. Behind the town hall, built in the form of a Greek temple, is the glass roof of the railroad station, from where goods manufactured in the factories on the skyline were sped to consumers both in Britain and abroad. Such buildings were erected as lasting monuments, and they still dominated the city long after the role of heavy industry in the local economy had declined.

the inconceivably rapid increase of immense towns under it, are without parallel in the history of the world.''

There would be plenty of parallels in the world's future. Europe and North America would be well along the same uncomfortable path to industrial development before the nineteenth century was over; by the end of the first half of the twentieth, much of the world would have experienced the mixed blessings of large-scale urbanization, and most of the rest would be in the throes of the transformation. Thus, in 1800, no city had more than one million inhabitants; by 1900, a dozen did. By the 1970s, at least 130 cities were that size; and two decades later, some of them had swollen into barely manageable conglomerations of 20 million or more.

Workers dressed in overalls stand in long production lines at an electric-motor assembly plant in Berlin in 1900.

THE INDUSTRIAL VORTEX

As the Industrial Revolution increased in pace, immigrants from the countryside flooded into the cities, lured by the attractions of work, wages, and new social opportunities. In 1810, for example, London became the first European city since imperial Rome to house one million inhabitants. Thirty years later, its population had doubled, and by the end of the century, it had quadrupled—a pattern followed by cities in many other parts of the world.

For those accustomed to a life on the land, work in the city was a poor substitute. Although the pay was usually higher, the hours were longer, and the threat of recession could make employment uncertain. And in place of the old variety of the agricultural year, there was now the remorseless regimentation of the machine. The tool had become master, and the Belfast shipyard workers in the background photograph here, hurrying to begin the day's toil in 1911, were part of a global army that marched in response to the factory siren.

The impact of industrialization affected not only the size but also the appearance of the world's cities. In 1933, the British travel writer Peter Fleming was able to say that "São Paolo is like Reading, only much farther away." The same dubious distinction could have been claimed by cities in countries as distant as Africa, India, China, and Japan. Whatever cultural differences cities retained, they all now shared the factories, offices, slums, and suburbs that were the indelible stamp of industry.

But, at the same time, while the cities of the underdeveloped world were moving as fast as they could to emulate those of the developed, their role models were abandoning the pattern they had set. And in a dramatic fashion. Whatever modification or evolution the city had undergone in the last 5,000 years of urban life, it had

In this 1872 print, kimono-clad women labor at the looms of a Tokyo silk factory. The West provided both machines and customers.

always been a center. Ur in 2000 BC had been a hub to which people flocked; so had London in 1850. But as the world approached the twenty-first century, the city was losing that importance. Staggering developments in both transportation and communications had turned the world into what some described as a global village, and that was precisely the direction urban life was taking. Rather than coming to the city, people were leaving it. Equipped with phone, fax, car, and computer, the modern work force could pick and choose its workplace. And more often than not, that workplace was in the country. If something astonishing had happened to Glasgow and similar cities during the nineteenth century, something even more astonishing was happening to them during the twentieth: They were becoming redundant.

No single factor created the world's first industrialized society in Britain, and no single factor would be responsible for its later counterparts elsewhere. Certainly, it depended on complex interactions across a whole web of development in which vast improvements to the nation's farming methods, manufacturing techniques, and transportation system each operated as both cause and effect. But the key to the explosive combination of economic, scientific, and social developments that together created an industrial revolution was human numbers.

Throughout the eighteenth century, Britain's population had risen steadily, largely as a result of continuous and occasionally dramatic progress in agricultural methods and technology. New methods and new crops—above all, the potato—improved both the quantity and the quality of the rural diet. But the improvements did not benefit everyone: High-yield farming demanded capital, and its land enclosures often reduced subsistence farmers to the status of dependent laborers. Although the food surpluses brought about a rise in rural population, the farming methods that created them often resulted in a decline in rural opportunity; and men and women in vast numbers sought their fortune elsewhere.

"Elsewhere," of course, meant in a town. There was nothing new about the drift of rural hopefuls toward urban centers. In fact, for most of history, no town could have existed without these newcomers: Crowding and poor sanitation inevitably brought epidemic disease, which meant that urban death rates were almost always much higher than those of the surrounding countryside, and virtually every town in the world required a steady trickle of immigration merely to keep its population stable, much less to increase it. In London, for example, deaths during the eighteenth century had outnumbered births by more than 600,000, a figure equivalent to two-thirds of the city's population in 1800. The pattern was universal, and it had nothing to do with industrialization: Figures from early nineteenth-century Sweden, still a rural society, showed a death rate of 22.3 per thousand in the countryside, rising to 34.4 in towns, and a shocking 45.1 in Stockholm, the nation's only large city.

Most towns, however, could offer attractions that compensated for the risk of fatal illness. Social opportunities were immeasurably greater than in the countryside: Although few immigrants could hope to make a fortune in commerce, distribution, or administration—the main occupations of any town before the Industrial Revolution—most people found a wider choice of marriage partners, for example. For those who did have money to spend, towns had shops and markets. Miserable housing apart—and the country hovels from which the new arrivals came were seldom much better and sometimes much worse than those they had in the city—urban life, by and large, was more interesting than the dismal routines of subsistence farming.

But there were limits to the possibilities of urban growth, and there always had been. Until the time of the Industrial Revolution, it was simply impossible to produce enough food or fuel, in the small area that poor transportation facilities allowed, to keep a vast urban population alive. There were exceptional cases. A great port like London or Amsterdam, or a river-fed capital like Paris, could stretch these limits; and ancient Rome, by devoting most of an entire empire's resources to its supply routes, had grown to more than one million people. But the maximum size of most cities was dictated by the amount of food that oxcarts and pack mules could supply from its immediate hinterland.

By the late eighteenth century, however, transportation systems in the British Isles had been improved as dramatically as agricultural yields: Canals and good turnpikes already linked much of the country, and within two generations, the first railroad network in the world would be laid. Although there was often hunger among the urban poor, there was little chance of outright famine. Large cities had become a possibility. Part cause and part effect, the steady trickle of immigration from country to town became a flood.

New farming methods greatly increased the push away from the land; new industries equally increased the pull of the towns. For there was more work to be had: The British economy was growing at record rates, particularly in the area of textile manufacture, where a whole succession of eighteenth-century inventions had greatly increased production. Sometimes, these textiles were produced in one of the new "manufactories," where a waterwheel or a steam engine powered machine spinners and looms, and the human work force had to learn a mechanical and entirely new work discipline. But many of the first textile factories were not in towns at all: Initially, water power was more important than steam, and early industrialists often built their mills on relatively remote mountainsides, where rushing streams could be relied upon to keep the wheels turning relentlessly, and cheap housing for workers could be constructed easily.

Where the first factories were situated mattered not a bit to those who went to the city in search of work. For if the factory was in the country, the goods it produced inevitably found their way to the town, and there was plenty of work to be had in their warehousing, finishing, packaging, and distribution. In fact, even as late as 1830, the center of urban industry was less likely to be a factory than a warehouse, supplying raw materials to a host of workers who finished them in their own homes. Cities such as Manchester, Leeds, and Halifax, for example, grew up primarily as exchange towns, sucking in the produce from scattered clothiers in the surrounding countryside and spewing it out again to myriad tiny sweatshops.

In principle, this was nothing new to rural families, who had often done a little weaving or spinning to add a few pennies to their tiny incomes. But, congregated in an expanding town, the sheer numbers of the immigrants made them a new phenomenon on the human social scene. Most people had always been subject to the whims of weather and harvest; now, massed together with no other means of support than the single skill they sold to a few employers—sometimes a monopoly employer—they were subject to the caprice of the market. In boom times, there would be food on the table and money for clothing and even furniture; when trade turned downward, in its incomprehensible cycle, the workers faced destitution. And nowhere was this more noticeable than in the workshop cities. Factory owners may have been just as sensitive to the economic climate as warehousers, but at least they had the motivation of a wasted capital investment to remain in production. For the warehousers and distributors, however, it was a simple matter to shift the burden of depression onto their casual, self-employed labor.

Just as the birth of a mass work force would have profound and permanent effects on social relationships and politics, so the place it lived in was rapidly transformed into a very new kind of city. As every observer noted, it was grossly overcrowded: Immigrants were arriving far faster than accommodations, even wretched accommodations, could be created for them. Initially, existing buildings were simply crammed with more people.

Glasgow's problems were particularly acute, but the city's experience was nevertheless typical. By 1800, the houses of the old commercial center—once the homes of lawyers and merchants—had been split up into scores of tiny apartments, with

Vienna's grandiose boulevard, the Ringstrasse, or Ring Road, clearly visible in this 1873 lithograph, was the brainchild of the Austro-Hungarian emperor Franz Josef I, who made room for it in 1857 by ordering the demolition of the city's medieval fortifications. Other European capitals, especially Paris, had launched ambitious redevelopment schemes, and the emperor was determined that Vienna should not be left behind.

The aristocracy continued to live in the old inner city, dominated by the thirteenth-century cathedral of Saint Stephen, while the working classes were pushed into the distant suburbs and industrial districts. The ring itself, a two and one-half mile loop extending from the Danube Canal, seen in the middle distance, was lined with lush gardens, lavishly designed public buildings, and fashionable middle-class apartments. A French visitor to Vienna in the 1880s was struck by the frantic imitation of all things Parisian. "Whatever people say, and whatever they do," he observed, "the influence of Paris reigns supreme, because it is the city of good taste, wealth, and the arts."

148

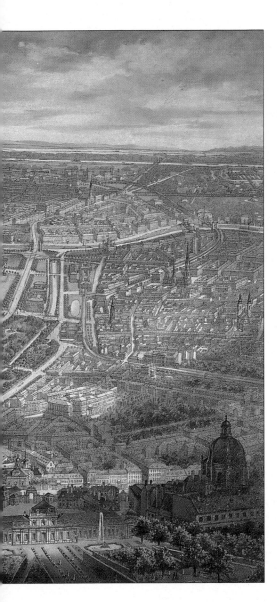

cheaply built new floors added, and yet more hovels constructed in what had once been gardens. A labyrinth of stinking alleyways—the "wynds" that so disgusted the 1839 commission—provided access, ventilation, and waste disposal alike. Later, specially built accommodations were not much better: A whole series of industrial villages were constructed around the old center, in which all the inhabitants of a crowded tenement were often engaged in the business of their landlord-employer—weaving, for example, or the associated trades of bleaching and dyeing.

Although these toilers were creating wealth on a scale never seen before, they enjoyed very little of it themselves. The irony was well expressed by the French historian Alexis de Tocqueville, who toured Manchester in 1835. Like most other visitors, he was both shocked and impressed by the place. Accustomed to France's traditions of state direction, he noted the good and bad effects of its absence: "At every turn, human liberty shows its capricious creative force. There is no trace of the slow continuous action of government." One result was the oozing slums he saw "surround the huge palaces of industry and clasp them in their hideous folds." But he also observed: "From this foul drain, the greatest stream of human industry flows out to fertilize the whole world. From this filthy sewer, pure gold flows. Here, humanity attains its most complete development and its most brutish; here, civilization works its miracles, and civilized man is turned back almost into a savage."

Those who had access to the gold seldom noticed the sewer, or cared much about the savagery. The American writer Nathaniel Hawthorne, appointed U.S. consul in the sprawling port of Liverpool in 1853, enthused about his own new quarters, recently constructed by a speculative builder. "It is a stone edifice, like almost all the modern English houses, and handsome in its design—much more so than most of the American houses," he wrote. Despite the vast increase in the city's population—it had doubled in size in the first three decades of the century—Hawthorne found his street "the quietest place imaginable; there being a police station at the entrance; and the officer on duty admits no ragged or ill-looking person to pass." It was not surprising that Hawthorne considered his lifestyle an "improvement on anything save what the very rich can enjoy in America."

As Hawthorne implied, such an existence, in industrializing Britain, was no longer the prerogative of the plutocrats. Although the huddled poor saw little of the riches their labor was producing, a thriving middle class—not just owners and capitalists, but managers, senior overseers, and the lawyers, doctors, and accountants who served them—was wealthier and more numerous than ever before. On the edge of all Britain's industrial cities there sprang up a ring of substantial dwellings, solidly constructed and often embellished with all the trimmings—of which there were plenty, for nineteenth-century wealth was not fussy about its source books—an architect could dream up.

The inhabitants of these dwellings themselves provided a massive source of employment. Large, ostentatious houses required a small army of domestic servants; and middle-class incomes also supported a whole chain of more or less lowly service trades, from dressmakers and milliners to chimney sweeps and waiters.

Between the lifestyles enjoyed at the top of the social heap and those endured at the bottom was a gulf as great as any that human society had seen. But the new urban rich and the new urban poor did have one thing in common: the city itself, and its dangers. For although good transport ensured that the cities of the Industrial Revolution could be free from famine, the risk of disease was as high as ever, and increasing every year. Early nineteenth-century Britain contained within its boundaries more large cities than had ever existed anywhere in history; but they seemed to be hardly more able than any of their predecessors to prevent the constant drain of deaths from sickness and the regular, scourging epidemics that were still the inevitable price of urban living.

Typhus, spread by ticks and fleas, was commonplace, as were tuberculosis, diphtheria, smallpox, and a host of contagious fevers, only a few of them firmly identified by contemporary medicine, which was quite incapable of treating them effectively. But these were no more than normal urban hazards, afflictions sent by an inscrutable deity, to be endured with resignation—especially since they were mostly endured by the luckless poor and their children.

The devastating arrival in 1831 and 1832 of cholera, hitherto exclusively an Asian sickness, was another matter entirely. Ironically, its appearance in Europe was mainly the result of an improved transportation network, a side effect of a developing global economy that allowed expanding cities to use the whole world as their hinterland.

Advertising posters cram the walls of London's Charing Cross station in 1874, an indication of rail travel's enormous popularity. Pioneered in Great Britain in the 1830s, the railroad was a vital factor in the country's industrial expansion. Cities competed to attract the new lines, and the vast glass roofs of railroad stations rose like the cathedrals of a new age. Despite early fears of the so-called firehorses—the sparks from the locomotives would occasionally set fire to fields and houses—the public clamored to travel by train. By 1851, Britain had more than 6,800 miles of track and an annual total of some 80 million rail passengers. Not everyone was pleased by these developments: The Duke of Wellington complained that railroads merely "enabled the lower orders to go uselessly wandering about the country."

But it was a very frightening side effect: A cholera victim could be in perfect health in the morning and a shriveled, blue-blotched corpse by nightfall. And although the era's doctors had no idea that cholera was caused by a waterborne bacillus, everyone could see that it did most of its killing among the overcrowded poor in their notoriously unsanitary slums. But it killed elsewhere, too; and it threatened everyone.

The British government, which prided itself on principles of laissez-faire and minimum state interference, was compelled by the spectacle of rapidly filling city graveyards to take action—of a sort. "Whereas it has pleased Almighty God to visit the United Kingdom with the disease called the cholera," began the preamble to Parliament's 1832 Cholera Act, "And whereas, with a view to prevent, as far as may be possible, by the divine blessing, the spreading of the said disease," Britain's legislators established unpaid district boards of health, on whom the responsibility for prevention would rest.

In the end, the boards achieved little, and not only because Parliament granted them few powers, and less money. Nineteenth-century medical science had no adequate theory of disease: Most doctors considered talk of germs to be superstitious nonsense and preferred to explain epidemic illness as the result of a "miasma" of infected air that arose from the earth itself. But most observers—the British government, unsure of how to handle its new cities, sent out inquiring commissioners by the score—reckoned there was a clear connection between urban filth and urban illness.

The answer lay under their noses. Despite the considerable improvements made to London's drains in the preceding century, they were no match for what the industrial multitudes sent their way. Numerous underprivileged families shared—and in some overcrowded districts actually slept in—privies that blocked to overflowing for months on end. Nor was the problem confined to poor areas: For all the above-ground glories of the capital's most prestigious residential squares, their clogged drains usually leaked a nauseating effluvium. It was impossible to clean many of the oldest sewers, lest the action remove the very filth that held them together. Those that were flushed simply sent their bacilli into the Thames River, thus contaminating the capital's main source of drinking water. And even when not choked, the pipes acted as conduits for hordes of disease-carrying rats who entered homes on nighttime foraging expeditions. Reports abounded of babies being attacked in their cribs.

Reformers and hydraulic engineers—in particular one Joseph Bazalgette, whose drainage work in Northern Ireland gained him a consultancy post with the London borough of Westminster in 1842—proposed radically new sanitation systems, in which drinking water and waste would be rigorously separated, and open sewers would be replaced by high-pressure underground piping, made from durable ceramics, that would carry effluent safely away. The work was well within the power of nineteenth-century technology, and the country's booming economy could certainly support the expense.

It was not until 1847, however, when reports from continental Europe made it clear that another "visitation" was imminent, that people seriously began to address the problem. The outcome was Britain's first Public Health Act in 1848, which became law only days before cholera erupted once more in British cities. The act, much resented by city landlords, was far from all-powerful, and the central health authority it established endured only a few years. But a critical beginning was made. In 1859, Bazalgette, now chief engineer of the London Metropolitan Commission for Sewers, started work on purging the capital's sordid intestines. And sixteen years later, 80 miles of new intercepting sewers bored through the ground under London, flushing the waste from some 100 square miles. Bazalgette's sewers were an example for the world, and it was not long before other industrial cities followed London's lead.

The consequences were dramatic. Urban death rates began to fall. In Glasgow, for example, deaths peaked at fifty-six per thousand in the epidemic year of 1847; by the 1870s, the rate had fallen to twenty-five. Since the birthrate in the same period hovered around forty per thousand, Glasgow was now growing steadily from its own resources—not from immigration, although this still continued. The statistics were similar elsewhere—in Britain itself and shortly afterward throughout Europe and the United States, where industrialization was spreading—and expanding cities, facing the same problems, adopted similar solutions.

Beyond their impact on urban hygiene, however, Bazalgette's sewers were clear evidence that government, both municipal and central, was taking seriously its responsibility to its citizens. Increasingly, basic facilities such as the supply of water and gas—just two opportunities for profit seized upon by often unscrupulous entrepreneurs—were coming under municipal control. And it was not just the basics: Public lighting, street paving, libraries, housing, hospitals, even laundries and baths were all being brought under the governmental aegis. In 1875, for example, Birmingham's mayor, Joseph Chamberlain, ordered the demolition and redevelopment of more than forty acres of slum dwellings, the whole project to be underwritten by the city coffers. As other municipal governments followed Chamberlain's paternalistic lead, the expression "city father" took on ever-greater meaning.

It was not just concern for their "children" that spurred Britain's authorities to introduce improvements. There was a growing pride in the wealth, efficiency, and productivity of the expanding cities, and urban elites were determined that their city should be better than those of their rivals. And not just *be* better, but *be seen* to be

Shoppers browse among the fruits of mass production, many imported, in Budapest's Paris department store in 1900. As the industrial middle classes prospered, conspicuous consumption became the order of the day. By the 1830s, Parisian merchants were exploiting the bourgeois gold mine with department stores and multiple retail chains whose variety, low prices, and convenience offered the ultimate shopping experience. Others were quick to follow. By the turn of the century, Budapest was the fastest-growing city in Europe, and the Paris was an accurate index of its affluence. The store even boasted electricity, although a fire started by a short circuit razed it in 1903.

better. The British textile center of Bradford, for example, chose the Venetian Doge's Palace as a model for its new town hall. Glasgow, in 1850, almost swamped by festering slums considered the worst in the country, tore down its entire city center and replaced it with an ebullient—and, for the time, typical—mix of Greek, Gothic, Renaissance, and baroque styles, often vying for attention in the same building. In most cases, the profits generated by the shops and offices in the reconstructed centers were more than enough to pay for redevelopment.

Town planning depended as much on the power of city authorities as it did on the desires of architects and citizens. Despite the large-scale reconstruction that had taken place in many cities during the eighteenth century, most city centers were old, and the legal rights of their property owners were as bewilderingly entangled as the streets and alleyways their buildings occupied. The construction of London's splendid Regent Street between 1813 and 1827, for example, had required an act of Parliament as well as considerable capital; even so, its sinuous curves owed as much to holdout landlords as to its architect's skill.

In Britain during the first decades of the nineteenth century, the structure of urban government was a shambles, a chaotic tangle of traditional vested interests that were narrow in outlook and unwilling to spend large sums. Only the emergence of a wealthy industrial class and the prompting of successive piecemeal legislation had enabled any improvements to be made to living conditions. The situation was different, however, on the Continent. In France, Germany, and Austria, there was an established tradition of strong, central rule, supplemented by bodies of professional municipal officials. And a generation after the construction of Regent Street, France's Emperor Napoléon III and his prefect of the Seine, Baron Georges-Eugène Haussmann, showed what an ambitious and authoritarian government, armed with vast powers of compulsory acquisition (and vast sums of borrowed money), could achieve. By 1870, they had virtually re-created Paris, replacing much of its congested old heart with wide, straight avenues, lined with shops and businesses whose earnings, the planners rightly guessed, made the whole immense project self-financing.

There was no doubt that civic improvements benefited almost everyone, but many ordinary workers still lived in less than palatial accommodations. In most places, the industrial work force itself was shrinking, as the methods of production became more efficient year by year and more people found employment in the increasingly complex service sectors—such as teaching and administration—that an advanced industrial economy demanded. But powerful class divisions still existed, and those toward the bottom of the social order usually paid a price for it, not just in restricted opportunities but in physical well-being.

Although adequate water supplies now protected cities from the fearful die-offs caused by epidemic disease, urban ailments, such as tuberculosis, still preyed on crowded townspeople. And although better transport systems were rushing food into the city, its presence was useless to those who could not afford it. The Victorian chronicler Henry Mayhew recorded the testimony of one young Londoner who sold watercress—"four bunches a penny"—for a living:

> I don't have no dinner. Mother gives me two slices of bread and butter and a cup of tea for breakfast, and then I go to tea, and has the same. . . . Mother has just the same to eat as we has, but she takes more tea—three cups sometimes.

The same kind of diet could have been found among the industrial poor in any country, and it was little wonder that Parisian military lists should have shown working-class military conscripts to be markedly smaller than middle-class recruits, or that Berlin archives should record, as late as 1880, an average lifespan of less than thirty years.

These conditions did not go noticed by officialdom only. Since Karl Marx and Friedrich Engels had published their *Communist Manifesto* in 1848, an as-yet infinitesimal but steadily growing number of workers were beginning to demand some share in the industrial politics that shaped their destinies. During the following century, their voices would be heard loud and clear. But for the moment, the prevailing mood was best captured by a citizen of Manchester, whom Engels harangued at length about the poor conditions in which his townspeople lived. ''The man listened quietly to the end and said at the corner where we parted: 'And yet there is a great deal of money to be made here; good morning, sir.' ''

The money that Engels's Mancunian and others were making was being put to good use. During the 1860s and 1870s, towns throughout Europe and the United States undertook grandiose schemes of reconstruction, many following the lead set by Haussmann in Paris. But civic change was not restricted to civic centers. In virtually every major city there now soared a vast, cathedral-like structure, beneath whose glass roof and cast-iron columns puffed the new arbiter of urban development: the steam locomotive.

Huddled beside an open sewer, Glasgow families pose for the camera in a center-city slum. The photograph was taken in 1868, at a time when half of the children born into these dark and fetid alleys died before they reached ten years of age, and the average life expectancy for the survivors was less than forty years. It was the same grim story in many industrial towns: Killer diseases such as typhoid, cholera, and tuberculosis swept through the unsanitary warrens into which many of the poorer citizens were crowded, and crime, drunkenness, and prostitution were rampant. It was not until late in the nineteenth century that the legislators, spurred by an outraged public, began to introduce minimum standards of health and safety.

Pioneered in Great Britain in 1830, rail travel had dramatically altered the pace of city life—quite literally, in Britain's case, where regional centers that had previously ticked to the tranquil pace of their own, uncoordinated, local times, had had to change their clocks to fit in with London's bustling schedules. More important, rail communications now dictated the shape of urban expansion. Humanity as well as goods surged along the iron arteries, and the opportunities that drew people to the city could be enjoyed from an ever-farther distance. Until 1850, almost everyone in the world, fieldworker and factory worker, walked to work, and the need to keep homes and workplaces in close proximity was one reason for the notorious overcrowding of the first industrial towns. But with the advent of steam locomotives, that crowding could be dissipated into the surrounding countryside. And as an increasing variety of mass transit was introduced—horse-drawn buses and streetcars, then electric streetcars, and finally, the electric railroad—the process was hastened still further.

The age of the suburb had arrived. As early as 1835, Manchester businesspeople had begun developing suburban villas ''free from any possible nuisances that may arise from the vicinity of smoke and manufactures; and to combine, with the advantage of a close proximity to the town, the privacy and advantage of a country residence.'' A few decades later, Paris, Berlin, and imperial Vienna had all acquired a thriving outer fringe.

Sometimes, the railroads connected existing settlements, absorbing them into a great metropolis. Such was the case in London—where by 1900, some five million people lived in what most of them regarded as a single city—and throughout much of Britain and continental Europe. In the United States, speculative rail and streetcar builders often drove new lines deep into empty countryside, buying up land cheaply and waiting, rarely for very long, for the parent city to send out a new tendril of growth, a phenomenon known as ribbon development, which would eventually join cities with their neighbors in vast, built-up conurbations in which the old idea of ''city limits'' made no real sense. Either way, it was obvious that urban transportation had become far more than a convenience. It was a vital, people-moving network that virtually defined the city it served.

The precise social pattern of cities varied from country to country. In British cities, the better-off tended to move outward to newly built residential suburbs, mostly constructed by speculative builders aware of the rising number of middle-class customers willing and eager to pay for a lifestyle that traded an increase in traveling time for an increase in living space; the civic centers were given over to commerce and surrounded by an inner ring of the overcrowded poor. Older U.S. cities—Boston and Philadelphia, for example—followed a similar pattern. In continental Europe, the reverse was often true. In Paris, for instance, Haussmann's boulevards made the historic center immensely attractive to the affluent, while the poorer classes were forced farther and farther outward into the *banlieue,* where a lucky few found comfortable suburbs, but most were condemned to live in dismal shantytowns. In Vienna and Berlin as well, workers' housing was pushed out and away from historic or rejuvenated centers.

By the dawn of the nineteenth century, the choice was no longer restricted to just city center or suburb. Urbanites could, if they wished, move to an entirely new, specially built, residential town, designed expressly with the convenience and comfort of its inhabitants in mind. The idea had first been theorized by a British industrialist named Robert Owen, whose philanthropy had led to the creation during the first two decades of the century of two ideal workers' communities: Scotland's New Lanark and the United States's New Harmony, Indiana. Here, he intended, the

The New York City skyline, dominated in this 1912 photograph by the sixty-story Woolworth Building, then the world's tallest, was most European immigrants' first view of the United States. Seen by many as the city of hope and opportunity, New York was a magnet to the poverty-stricken masses on the other side of the Atlantic Ocean: In 1902, its Ellis Island immigrant station was processing 8,000 arrivals a day. Newcomers who remained in the city, however, were usually crammed into decaying tenements with enormous population densities and hideous death rates. By the beginning of the twentieth century, New York had possibly the most congested housing on earth. For many Europeans, conditions were far worse than those they had left behind.

impersonal evils of industrial life would be held at bay. The town would provide work, adequate housing, schooling, entertainment—all the necessities of life encapsulated under the paternalistic umbrella of one single provider. Owen's vision was before its time. Financial difficulties led to the prompt disappearance of New Harmony and the slower, but inevitable, withering of New Lanark. But the seed had been sown. And in the second half of the century, while urban reformers published their plans in books with hopeful titles such as *Freeland* and *The Happy Colony,* Britain's hard-headed industrialists put their theories into practice.

To the ear, the resulting towns bore all the imprints of industrialism: Port Sunlight was concrete testimony to the cleansing power of Sunlight soap, while Bournville shared its name with the Cadbury family's leading brand of chocolate. But to the eye, they were dramatic departures from the standard concept of urban life. Detached or semidetached houses, half-timbered and gabled, nestled amid gardens, treelined roads, parks, and recreation areas in an almost villagelike atmosphere.

Town planning, hitherto the hobby of a few fortunate monarchs or the outcome of laissez-faire economics, was becoming an organized discipline, best exemplified at the turn of the century by the idea of the garden city, which arose almost simultaneously in the United States and Britain. A reaction against the urban nightmares of industrialization, the garden city was almost antiurban in concept: a community whose numbers and self-contained industries were deliberately limited, and most of whose area was given over to green space in what the idea's English exponent Ebenezer Howard described as a combination of town and country "in which all the advantages of the most energetic and active town life, with all the beauty and delight of the country, may be secured in perfect combination." The idea caught the popular imagination, and garden cities, or variations on the theme, proliferated during the first ten years of the twentieth century. In 1902, when England's Garden City Association was founded, Germany responded with its Deutsche Gartenstadtgesellschaft. Ten years later, when plans for two garden capitals, New Delhi in India and Canberra in Australia, were unveiled, it seemed as if a new way of urban life was truly possible.

During the first decade of the twentieth century, life in the cities of Europe and North America was better than it had ever been before. Improved sewers had led to a dramatic improvement in civic health, and freed for the first time from the ancient curse of epidemic disease, city-bred people could exist not only in large but in growing numbers. There was more and better housing to shelter the new multitudes, and at the same time, more food to place on their tables—steam locomotives enabled perishable supplies to be imported both from around the country and, after the development of refrigeration systems in the 1870s, from the vast plains of the New World. The streets were lighted at night, the roads were well paved, and even in the most adamantly industrial of towns, reformist planners were constructing parks and open green spaces for the physical and mental well-being of the inhabitants. There were more police to apprehend criminals and—following the development in America of multistory, galleried prisons—more places to keep them. There was more of everything: more money, more jobs, a wider range of goods to buy, a larger number of shops to buy them in, and more people who could buy them. And if many people still simply endured the city, there were an equal number who actively enjoyed it.

The move toward a life of urban leisure, already begun in the eighteenth century, had received new impetus from an increasingly wealthy middle class. The rawness

American typists of the early 1900s transcribe letters from converted Edison phonographs, the first office dictating machines. The mechanization of office procedures—sparked in the 1870s by the typewriter, the telephone, and the adding machine—presented middle-class women with a vast new range of job opportunities. Previously, most of the paperwork had been handled by correspondence clerks, male employees whose copperplate handwriting earned them an elevated position in the office hierarchy. It was soon discovered, however, that typists could produce letters much more quickly—and that women could be paid half the wages.

of early industrial cities began to disappear as bars, cafés, theaters, operas, music halls, and beginning with the first decade of the twentieth century, movies sprang up for the amusement of the populace. High society, as usual, led the way. During the three summer months of London's "season," for example, the capital became a frenzy of balls, receptions, and parties as the nation's nobility—clutching manuals on etiquette such as *A Member of the Aristocracy* or *The Gentleman in the Club Window,* which were written by anonymous social authorities—poured in from country estates to hobnob with their peers. The same held true for Paris, Vienna, Saint Petersburg, and New York City.

The fun was restricted neither to capital cities nor to the upper classes. Though wretchedly small in comparison to the sums their employers were earning, workers' paychecks were nevertheless far bigger then they had ever been before. And with this newly acquired wealth, they could enjoy what would have been unheard of 100 years earlier: a vacation.

Steam travel had enormously expanded humanity's horizons, and enterprising Americans had been the first to appreciate the profits to be made out of the transient masses. "The American hotel is to an English hotel what an elephant is to a periwinkle," one admiring nineteenth-century Briton had remarked as early as 1866. But by the dawn of the twentieth century, virtually every major city in the world had large hotels—the most prestigious bearing the name of César Ritz, a Swiss-born hotelier—whose occupants were usually there for pleasure rather than for business.

The development phenomenon was not restricted to single buildings. As early as the eighteenth century, canny developers had realized that the liverish rich liked to

157

In this 1859 painting, harassed London bus passengers come under the baleful scrutiny of a top-hatted conductor. The rudeness of bus crews was a constant source of complaint.

New Yorkers take the el during an evening rush hour in 1912. Although these elevated railroads could be built without demolishing property, most cities preferred the less-obtrusive subway system.

MOVING THE MULTITUDES

Public transportation within the city was almost unknown before the nineteenth century. However, as towns expanded, it became necessary to bridge the gap between the home and the workplace. The first vehicle to do so was the horse-drawn bus, introduced in Paris in 1819.

Competition between the bus companies was fierce, and few scruples were shown by their crews. According to Charles Dickens, a London conductor "could tell at a glance where a passenger wanted to go, and would shout the name of the place accordingly, without the slightest reference to the real destination of the vehicle."

In the 1830s, the horse-drawn trolley appeared in New York City. Running on smooth rails rather than on the rough road, it was much easier to haul than a standard bus. This gave operators the chance to increase passenger loads and charge lower fares than their bus rivals.

In the 1880s, again in New York, the horse-drawn trolley began to give way to the electric streetcar, and in the early 1900s, this in turn was challenged by the motorbus. Regarded at first as a fume-belching novelty, it was to become the most popular means of urban transportation until the age of the automobile.

As congestion increased on the roads, overground and underground railroads were built to relieve the strain. The first underground line, served by steam trains, was opened in London in 1863. With the advent of electric trains in the 1890s, the system was greatly improved, and other cities soon had subways of their own.

Taxis, horse-drawn buses, electric streetcars, and autos converge at a busy Paris intersection in 1910. Such congestion had led to the introduction of traffic signals during the 1890s.

Large windows and gas lamps light the interior of London's Baker Street station, opened in 1863 as part of the first underground railroad. The line was less inviting, and travelers called it the sewer.

take the waters and had built spa towns to attract the trade. And now, whole cities—Blackpool, Monte Carlo, Atlantic City—existed solely for the purpose of entertaining vacationers. Whether in the genteel atmosphere of the pump room, around the gaudy lights of a seaside pier, or in the headily expensive environs of some wedding-cake casino, throngs of merrymakers were breathing life into a new breed of city.

For five years, however, from 1914 to 1919, it was a bloody tour in the trenches rather than a sunny break by the sea that broke the monotony of industrial toil. The lustrum of carnage that seized Europe toppled the old order that had so gaily flocked capitalward for their entertainment and social diversions; and at the end of World War I, it was a sterner, increasingly socialist rule that prevailed. When Britain's prime minister avowed his determination at the end of hostilities "to make Britain a fit country for heroes to live in," most European leaders harbored similar ambitions.

Throughout the Continent—particularly in the war-shattered shards of the Russian, German, and Austrian empires—slums were torn down and public housing projects put in their place. Some were little more than clusters of dwellings that, for all the good intention behind them, were dark and airless, as if what had gone before set the standard of things to come. Others were veritable palaces of the people, whose heroic facades and leafy courtyards looked forward to a more egalitarian future. But whatever the outcome of the planners' designs, they signaled the entrenchment of one important principle of urban life. An influx of people had created the city; it was now the city's inescapable duty to provide for them.

It took longer for concepts of civic responsibility to pervade North America, that vast pool of opportunity where the benefits of industrialism were reserved mostly for those who swam rather than those who sank. Since the 1880s, urban life across the Atlantic Ocean had been epitomized by the skyscraper, from whose heights the successful could congratulate themselves on how far they had risen above the squalid tenements in the streets below. Furthermore, the United States was a big place. Unlike Europe, where the urban poor had effectively nowhere to go—except, perhaps, if they could afford the fare, to America itself—citizens of the United States could move out to make their fortunes elsewhere on the continent. And no area was more popular than the sunny, undeveloped West Coast. In 1880, for example, the population of Los Angeles had been 11,000; ten years later, it had risen to 50,000; and by 1930, there were more than two million Angelenos. And the city they lived in was unlike any that the world had seen before.

The cities of the whole Atlantic region of Europe and of the eastern United States, whatever their individual differences, shared certain common characteristics. Some were many centuries old; all had begun their population growth before the development of urban transportation systems; and, however much they had expanded, they remained dense agglomerations within which land was always very expensive, and buildings, even in the suburbs, were pressed closely together. But in the American West, which scarcely two generations before had been an empty wilderness, there were few space constraints. And whereas the modern existence of most of the East Coast cities had begun with the pressing need to accommodate enormous numbers of low-paid workers, the new western cities were more service oriented and tended from their inception to have a more even distribution of income. Climate was an equally important factor: There was far less need to heat dwellings in California than in the chilly New England states or in northern Europe, and hence, there was no advantage for even poor people to huddle together into the smallest possible space.

The result—Los Angeles was the archetype, but similar developments appeared as far apart as Melbourne in Australia and Buenos Aires in Argentina—scarcely seemed a city at all, at least not to eyes accustomed to Hamburg, London, Pittsburgh, or New York. Instead of traditional streets and high-rise apartments, there was a vast sprawl of endless suburbs punctuated by a few small commercial centers, with industry scattered, seemingly at random, throughout the area.

These were twentieth-century cities par excellence, and almost from their birth, the nature of their growth was determined by the twentieth century's dominant means of transportation: the automobile. Since Henry Ford's Model T first rolled off his Detroit factory's conveyor belts in 1913, the United States had led all industrialized nations in both the production and ownership of automobiles. By 1929, there were already 27 million cars on American roads, far more than in the remainder of the world. World War II, with its immense increases in output and its scattering of industrial enterprise (and the government largesse that funded them) over the entire country, accelerated the trend toward the extended city. Fast, reliable personal transportation linked people, goods, and services across larger and larger distances, granting to vast areas the kind of immediacy of communication that had hitherto been possible only in traditionally dense urban centers. And with the wealth and technology of the world's most powerful economy at hand, the new-style cities could spring up just about anywhere. By the 1970s, the urbanization of large tracts of American desert was well under way.

Paradoxically, the automobile had precisely the opposite effect on older cities, to whose traditional lifestyle it was anathema. In 1900, traffic had flowed through New York City's streets at a respectable eleven miles an hour. By 1960, the congestion created by several million cars had reduced speeds to less than six. In effect, the same machine that had shrunk the 464 square miles of Los Angeles into a virtual urban center had doubled the size of the once-compact eastern metropolis and drastically reduced its civic efficiency.

European cities lagged significantly behind in the automobile revolution. The Continent's far denser population obviously restricted the large-scale road building that made the American experience possible. More immediately, though, World War II brought Europe not prosperity but disaster. Many of its major cities lay in utter ruin, and it was decades before rebuilding was complete. By the 1970s and 1980s, however, car ownership in Western Europe was approaching American levels, with similar effects: Cities were being steadily strangled by their own vehicles, both metaphorically, in the sense of traffic congestion, and literally, too, from the ceaseless output of poisonous fumes whose miasma—nineteenth-century doctors would have appreciated it—choked people and corroded buildings.

Traditional city life, it seemed, was more resistant to bombs and artillery than to automobiles. For although technologists could refine and purify damaging exhaust fumes—by the 1990s, most developed countries were enforcing increasingly strict controls—it was the social effects of mass car ownership that threatened to change cities forever. Ever since steam locomotives had spurred the first ribbon development, cities had spread themselves to follow transportation links. Millions of automobiles amounted not so much to a link, or links, as to a huge, diffuse cloud of potential communication that drifted around existing urban centers. A city was no longer required in order to supply what cities had provided in the past—trade and com-

An underground-railroad poster of 1908 promotes the prim delights of Golders Green, one of London's earliest suburbs. To those anxious to escape the noise, dirt, and tumult at the heart of the capital, the neat gardens and mock-Tudor houses of suburbia were a sanctuary. Offering the fresh air and green spaces of the country, yet only a short train ride from the city, they seemed to combine the best of both worlds. Similar developments occurred in continental Europe and in the United States, where one enthusiast looked forward to the disappearance of the traditional city and its replacement by a "federation of communities coordinated into a metropolis of sunlight and air."

UNDERGROUND ARTERIES

The modernity of any city may be measured by the services—heating, lighting, telephones, air conditioning—that its inhabitants take for granted. Cities, by promoting high standards of living, have themselves created the demand for such amenities; but as pressure on space has increased, so have the problems of those charged with supplying the cities' needs.

The engineers of ancient Rome took pride in the aqueducts that carried water from the surrounding hills to supply the city's baths and fountains and to flush out its underground sewers, some of which are still in use today. But Rome was a magnificent exception: Most early cities relied on rivers for both water and waste disposal. For centuries, tainted and irregular water supplies and the stench of ordure in the streets were inescapable features of urban life, and it was not until the sudden increase of populations in the industrialized cities of the West in the nineteenth century that planners and engineers seriously began to tackle the problems of sanitation.

Between 1840 and 1880, many Western cities acquired new water supplies and work was begun on underground sewers.

Such measures reduced cholera outbreaks and greatly improved the quality of urban life. At the same time, however, new technologies placed an increasing burden on supply systems. Gas street lighting was introduced early in the century; from about 1880, electricity provided a more efficient form of energy, while telephones revolutionized communications.

Underground labyrinths of cables and pipes were progressively expanded to meet the new needs and expectations of city dwellers. The reconstruction on the right shows a typical pattern of services. Running parallel to one another under the road, the main water, gas, and electricity supplies are connected at intervals to distribution systems under the pavement. Foul water from buildings and drains is disgorged into a combined sewer; at a lower level, a storm sewer takes surface water; inspection chambers provide access for repairs. In some countries, these services are supplemented by the provision of compressed air to drive machinery and steam for central heating. Invisible above ground, these are the vital life-support systems of any modern city.

Electricity

Gas

Waste

Water

Telephone

merce, culture and industry, homes and society, work and play. Little subcities—that is, buildings or groups of people performing various hitherto urban functions—could and did exist in scattered pockets throughout the open land. The division between city and countryside, as clear two centuries before as the division between land and sea, was coming to an end.

Further advances seemed to be hastening the process. The red glow of the industrial furnace had now been replaced by what Britain's prime minister Harold Wilson described in the 1960s as "the white heat of technology." Ever since the late nineteenth century, telephones had brought people together, albeit in a limited way. One hundred years later, a tidal wave of development in electronics, miniaturization, and telecommunications made possible massive exchanges of complex information, cheaply and across global distances. Such connectivity made only a modest difference to the manufacturing industry: Workers in a steel mill, for example, still had to labor side by side in order to produce the goods by which they earned their living. But "work" in an advanced economy in the late twentieth century was more likely to mean the providing of services, distribution, and administration, for example, than manufacturing. Often, this work could be done perfectly well by widely separated people linked only by the copper wire, optical fibers, and satellite relays that exchanged packets of electronic data between them. These people could live almost anywhere as citizens of as many overlapping "electronic cities" as they liked.

Real working cities, too, could be built almost anywhere—at least by the world's most advanced economies. Energy distribution that had once involved the shortest possible rail link to the nearest possible coal mine now meant no more than a power line tapping into a national energy network. No area benefited more from the increased mobility of both people and energy than the sunbelt cities of the southwestern United States. Attracted by the warm, dry climate, people by the hundred thousand could transfer themselves and their workplaces from a grimy older city in the North to a newly constructed city in the sun in what had once been an empty land. Phoenix, Arizona, for example, grew in an even more startling manner than its legendary namesake, for it sprang up from naked desert, while the ashes of its origin remained far off: Its people and industry alike came from the distant and decaying industrial cities of an earlier generation—the so-called rust belt.

Many traditional cities suffered serious problems as the result of such large-scale emigration, of which the most worrying was the phenomenon of the inner city, the district between the still-functioning commercial center and the more desirable outskirts. Deteriorating buildings, inhabited by a high proportion of unemployed people, tended to deteriorate still further, while their inhabitants—sometimes from a minority group and often recent newcomers to the city itself—seemed to be degenerating into a dangerous underclass. With nothing to gain from city life, and no means of escaping it, they had little to lose by riot and crime.

But since the time of ancient Rome or even before, cities had always had an underclass, and the more prosperous had always feared it. The police station at the end of Nathaniel Hawthorne's street of comfortable houses, back in 1853 Liverpool, had been built precisely to keep the underclass at bay. Over the span of a generation or two, most of the disadvantaged classes had been absorbed into mainstream urban life; and, in general, most cities had managed to endure a certain number of hopeless malcontents without disaster.

And despite all the changes to the pattern of urban life and the dispersal of urban

Viewed from the air, the freeways of Los Angeles snake through the land like concrete rivers. America's third-largest city grew by absorbing neighboring communities, such as Beverly Hills and Santa Monica, and is now a sprawling, centerless mass, seemingly held together only by its highways. Large tracts of land are devoted to freeways or parking lots, and the exhaust of internal-combustion engines exacerbates the area's notorious smog. Despite a mass transit system in the Los Angeles metropolitan area, the automobile reigns supreme. Only in L.A. could a planning report conclude with the comment that the "pedestrian remains as the largest single obstacle to free traffic movement."

functions, the cities of the advanced economies were still successful. New Yorkers might complain of their dangerous level of street crime, but those who could still paid high and rising prices to live there; the same was true of most other urban centers. For whatever the desirability of the semirural life that automobiles, commuting, and finally, electronics had made possible for so many, the city itself—its culture, its distinctive ethos, and its sheer excitement—remained an irresistible attraction to many more. Compared to the social problems of the early industrial age, the difficulties of the late twentieth century were modest. No one had ever solved all the problems then, and it was unlikely that anyone would solve every urban problem in the future. But as long as enough people still wanted to live in a city, those problems that could not be overcome would be endured.

While the world's most advanced cities pondered the possibilities of urban breakdown, some of the cities of the Third World were dangerously close to experiencing it in reality. Their difficulties, though, were not caused by urban abandonment, but by uncontrolled urban growth, which was faster and involved far more people than even the most traumatic developments in industrialized Europe.

At the root of the problem was the inability of Third World countries—whether through lack of resources, inadequate organization, or simple unpreparedness—to sustain the delicate balance between supply and demand of labor that industrial economics required. The Western technology that arrived in Latin America, Africa, and Asia during the nineteenth century intruded for the most part on societies that were predominantly agricultural, whose members survived on land that was often poor and subject to disasters such as flood and drought. For centuries, these populations had had a high birthrate, at least in part because the vicissitudes of climate and low crop yields claimed many children at an early age. But with the advent of Western technology—and particularly, following World War II, of Western medicine—the survival rate soared. And like all children of progress, the surplus farm hands flocked to the metropolitan areas. What they found there, however, was not the opportunity that had greeted their North American and European counterparts. In many cases, bad economic management coupled with civil war led to a decline in industrial capacity; single-product economies, developed to serve the needs of imperial powers, were particularly vulnerable to worldwide recessions; and even when there was economic growth, it was unable to cope with the tremendous demands of a burgeoning population.

The urban crisis arose in its most acute form during the 1970s, often in cities with a centuries-long record of civic continuity. The Indian megalopolis of Bombay, for example, was the richest and most successful city in Asia until the industrialization of Japan. British imperialism denied it self-government, but the British Empire gave it an open window onto the world economy, and trade and industry thrived. Cotton mills sprang up, often with Indian rather than British owners, and as early as 1860, a local newspaper could boast that "Bombay has long been the Liverpool of the East, and she is now become the Manchester also." Industry was as powerful a magnet to the Indian peasant as it was to the British: When Bombay's British-style chamber of commerce was founded in 1836, the city had 236,000 people; 60 years later, there were more than 800,000, some 75 percent of whom had been born outside the city. Although Bombay never attained European levels of hygiene (more than 100,000 died in a plague epidemic in the 1890s), increasing medical knowledge made it almost as healthy as its surrounding countryside, and like its European counterparts, it began to grow from its own resources.

But the rural population was growing even faster, especially after Indian independence in 1947, and immigration increased. By 1971, Bombay's population of nearly six million could no longer be accommodated even on the streets, where many of its homeless slept. Squatters built shantytowns around the city's edge, encircling the city with a ring of utter poverty. By the 1980s, its population was approaching nine million and still growing; for many, the only hope of survival was by begging from those who had little more themselves. And Bombay, with its long civic tradition, its bustling commerce, and its still-successful industries, was very far from being the world's most afflicted city.

In 1952, Lima, Peru, was a clean, attractive garden city of 700,000. By 1990, it had coalesced with nearby Callao into a huge urban sprawl that some estimates reckon—there were no accurate counts—embraced six million people, almost one-third of Peru's population. About two million lived in squatters' shanties; life for most of the rest was little better. Rural misery, increased by political unrest and terrorism, brought new squatters every day, seeking, like their predecessors, any kind of work that would keep starvation at bay. The old city center became bandit territory; the affluent found shelter in defended enclaves, while their ragged fellow citizens struggled with one another for survival. It had become a dreadful paradigm for city life in a poor land in the late twentieth century.

The same desperate shantytowns, built from refuse—flattened tin cans, cardboard boxes, pieces of straw—encroached on most of the great cities of the Southern Hemisphere. They were not always hopeless places—hope, in fact, was what drew most of their inhabitants from their country villages in the first place—and in a sense, they were examples of the same "capricious creative force" that de Tocqueville saw in Manchester 150 years earlier, when he lamented the absence of "the slow continuous action of government." But if the quality of misery was similar, the quantity was very much greater, beyond the power of any Third World government action, slow or otherwise, to help. The "filthy sewer" was present; but it would take some help from the successful cities of the developed world, the agony of their own unplanned growth now far behind them, to pass on something of the "pure gold" that de Tocqueville's Manchester possessed as compensation.

Packed together like the soldiers of some vast army, Tokyo window-shoppers make their way through the city's fashion district. Containing more than one-fourth of the nation's inhabitants, and with a population density as high as 22,275 people per square mile, the Japanese capital has become an insatiable megacity in which daily life is a continuous struggle for elbowroom. So great is the rush-hour crush on the trains and buses that limbs are sometimes broken and windows shattered. But for all its congestion, Tokyo at least has the technology to cope—unlike some Third World capitals whose faltering economies are often unable to sustain their soaring populations.

	4000-1000 BC	1000 BC-AD 500

During the early first millennium BC, Greece's rural population coalesces into city-states.

Democracy is born in the city-state of Athens (507 BC).

Greek colonists spread the orderly grid pattern of Hippodamean town planning around the Mediterranean.

Roman legionaries turn the Mediterranean region and most of Europe into an empire centered on Rome, which in the first century BC becomes the world's first city of one million people.

Rome is sacked by barbarian tribes (AD 410), leaving the eastern capital of Constantinople as the center of imperial power.

EUROPE

Olmec civilization arises in Central America (1200 BC).

The Maya become Central America's prime city builders (AD 300).

THE AMERICAS

The world's first civilization, Sumer, arises in southern Mesopotamia (c. 3500 BC).

Cities grow up along the Nile River in a united Egyptian kingdom ruled from Memphis (c. 3200 BC).

The pharaoh Djoser builds Egypt's first pyramid (c. 2650 BC).

Sumer's scattered cities are united under King Sargon (2334 BC); Ur becomes capital of a Sumerian empire that covers all of Mesopotamia.

Alexandria is founded at the mouth of the Nile River (332 BC). Under Alexander the Great, the Greek urban model is spread throughout the Middle East and Egypt.

Greek settlements in the Middle East fall under Roman sway.

As Rome declines, its eastern possessions come under the rule of Constantinople (c. AD 330).

THE MIDDLE EAST AND AFRICA

In India's Indus Valley, substantial urban developments arise around the cities of Mohenjo-Daro and Harappa (c. 2500 BC).

China's emergent civilization is united under the Shang dynasty (c. 1500 BC).

Supported by abundant rice harvests, cities cluster along India's Ganges Valley (c. 800 BC).

Alexander the Great brings Greek urban influence to northern India (326 BC).

ASIA AND THE FAR EAST

TimeFrame 4000 BC-AD 1990

500-1500	1500-1800	1800-1990

By 800, following the disintegration of Roman civilization, Europe's only thriving cities are Constantinople in the East and those of Muslim-occupied Spain in the West.

Europeans begin to gather for safety in fortified settlements, or burgs, which become the nuclei of larger, walled cities.

After the sacking of Constantinople (1204), Venice emerges as Europe's leading mercantile power.

From the fourteenth century, prosperous Italian cities of the Renaissance begin to remodel themselves along classical lines.

Henry IV remodels Paris as a royal capital (c. 1600). Other monarchs and governments also redesign their capitals to reflect the growing power of their nations: Wide boulevards and classical vistas replace the old huddle of medieval buildings.

After a disastrous fire (1666), London is rebuilt by architect Christopher Wren according to classical ideals.

Louis XIV establishes his administrative center at the newly built palace of Versailles, just outside Paris (1682).

Work starts on constructing a new Russian capital at Saint Petersburg (1703).

As the Industrial Revolution spreads through the Western world, cities increase dramatically in size and complexity. London becomes modern Europe's first city of one million people in 1810.

The plight of the urban proletariat prompts Karl Marx to publish the *Communist Manifesto* (1848).

Bazalgette's sewers in London become a showpiece for municipal hygiene (1875).

Planners seek a new form of urban life with the garden city (c. 1900).

Technological advances enable workers to leave increasingly congested cities in favor of a rural life.

North America's earliest towns are built in the Mississippi region (700).

The Incas found their capital of Cuzco in the Peruvian Andes (c. 1300).

The Aztecs set up a central American empire with their capital at Tenochtitlán, on the site of present-day Mexico City (1345).

After the overthrow of both the Aztec and Inca empires (1519-1534), Spain builds European-style cities throughout its Latin American empire.

French colonists found Quebec (1608).

Dutch settlers found New Amsterdam, modern New York City (1624).

Work starts on Washington, D.C., a specially built American capital designed according to classical Greek and Roman ideals (1793).

Immigration and the impact of the Industrial Revolution create huge, wealthy cities throughout the United States.

Chicago, the Midwest's major trading center, gives birth to the skyscraper (1885).

The advent of the automobile turns West Coast cities such as Los Angeles into vast sprawls of freeways and suburbs.

The specially built city of Brasília becomes capital of Brazil (1960).

Mexico City, surrounded by shantytowns, becomes the world's most populous city with 20 million inhabitants (1990).

Roman cities begin to decay as constant wars weaken Constantinople's grip.

By 640, Muslim armies have overrun classical civilization throughout the Middle East.

Baghdad is founded as capital of the Muslim empire (762).

With the fall of Baghdad to the Mongols, Cairo becomes Islam's preeminent city (1258).

As imperial powers colonize Africa in the late nineteenth century, European-style cities are built throughout the continent.

Muslim cities slowly yield to the technological changes of the industrial world. Ultramodern cities in Arabia mark that region as the world's oil center.

Changan, capital of the Tang dynasty, boasts one million inhabitants (c. 700).

The city of Kyōto, built according to Chinese cosmological principles, is founded as the capital of Japan (794).

Delhi rises to prominence as capital of a Muslim empire in northern India (1206).

English traders found Calcutta (1690). Like other Indian colonial centers, it is developed according to the classical pattern favored by Europeans.

China cedes to Britain the island of Hong Kong (1842), which rapidly becomes the richest trading center in the Far East.

Work begins on New Delhi, India's showpiece capital (1912).

As industrialism reaches the Far East, major centers such as Tokyo and Shanghai become increasingly westernized.

ACKNOWLEDGMENTS

The following materials have been reprinted with the kind permission of the publishers: Page 37: "Slavery . . ." quoted in *The Greek Way*, by Edith Hamilton, London: Dent, 1930. Page 44: "As a result . . ." quoted by permission of the publishers and the Loeb Classical Library from *Agricola* by Tacitus, transl. by M. Hutton, revised by R. M. Ogilvie, Cambridge, Massachusetts: Harvard University Press, 1970.

The editors also wish to thank the following individuals and institutions for their valuable assistance in the preparation of this volume:

England: Cambridge—Henry Hurst, Museum of Classical Archaeology. Chipping Norton, Oxfordshire—Stephen Ball. London—James Chambers; Brent Elliott, Librarian, Royal Horticultural Society; James Harpur; Elizabeth Harris, Lecturer in South and Southeast Asian History, School of Oriental and African Studies, University of London; London Transport Museum; Ferdie McDonald; John McNulty, Principal Engineer, London Borough of Fulham and Hammersmith; Jackie Matthews; Deborah Pownall.

BIBLIOGRAPHY

BOOKS

Abrams, P., and E. A. Wrigley, eds., *Towns in Societies.* Cambridge: Cambridge University Press, 1978.

Abu-Lughod, Janet L., *Cairo: 1001 Years of the City Victorious.* Princeton: Princeton University Press, 1971.

Alberti, Leone Battista, *Ten Books on Architecture.* London: Alec Tiranti, 1955.

Allchin, Bridget, and Raymond Allchin, *The Rise of Civilization in India and Pakistan.* Cambridge: Cambridge University Press, 1982.

Austin, M. M., ed., *The Hellenistic World from Alexander to the Roman Conquest.* Cambridge: Cambridge University Press, 1981.

Austin, M. M., and P. Vidal-Naquet, eds., *Economic and Social History of Ancient Greece.* London: Batsford, 1977.

Balazs, Etienne, *Chinese Civilization and Bureaucracy.* Ed. by Arthur F. Wright. Transl. by H. M. Wright. New Haven: Yale University Press, 1967.

Baldry, H. C., *Ancient Greek Literature in its Living Context.* London: Thames and Hudson, 1968.

Bassermann, Lujo, *The Oldest Profession.* Transl. by James Cleugh. London: Arthur Barker, 1967.

Bautier, Robert-Henri, *The Economic Development of Medieval Europe.* London: Thames and Hudson, 1971.

Beier, A. L., and R. Finlay, *The Making of the Metropolis: London 1500-1700.* London: Longman, 1986.

Benevolo, Leonardo, *The History of the City.* Transl. by Geoffrey Culverwell. London: Scolar Press, 1980.

Bishop, Morris, *The Horizon Book of the Middle Ages.* London: Cassell, 1969.

Boyd, Andrew, *Chinese Architecture and Town Planning 1500 B.C.-A.D. 1911.* London: Alec Tiranti, 1962.

Braudel, Fernand, *Civilization and Capitalism: 15th-18th Century.* Vols. 1, 2, and 3. Transl. by Siân Reynolds. London: Collins, 1981, 1982, 1984.

Browning, Iain, *Jerash and the Decapolis.* London: Chatto & Windus, 1982.

Brucker, Gene Adam:
Florence 1138-1737. London: Sidgwick & Jackson, 1984.
Renaissance Florence. Berkeley: University of California Press, 1983.

Bulliet, Richard W., *The Camel and the Wheel.* Cambridge, Massachusetts: Harvard University Press, 1975.

Burckhardt, Titus, *Art of Islam.* London: World of Islam Festival Publishing, 1976.

Burke, Gerald, *Towns in the Making.* London: Edward Arnold, 1971.

Carcopino, Jérôme, *Daily Life in Ancient Rome.* Ed. by Henry T. Rowell. Transl. by E. O. Lorimer. London: Penguin Books, 1962.

Chadwick, George F., *The Park and the Town.* London: Architectural Press, 1966.

Chambers, D. S., *The Imperial Age of Venice: 1380-1580.* London: Thames and Hudson, 1970.

Chamoux, François, *The Civilization of Greece.* Transl. by W. S. Maguinness. London: Allen & Unwin, 1965.

Chang Kwang-chih, *The Archaeology of Ancient China.* New Haven: Yale University Press, 1986.

Cheng Te-K'un, *Archaeology in China.* Cambridge: W. Heffer, 1959.

Cherry, Gordon, *Urban Change and Planning.* Henley-on-Thames, England: G. T. Foulis, 1972.

Chesney, Kellow, *The Victorian Underworld.* London: Temple Smith, 1970.

Clark, Grahame, *World Prehistory in New Perspective.* Cambridge: Cambridge University Press, 1977.

Coulton, G. G.:
A Medieval Garner. London: Constable, 1910.
Medieval Panorama. Cambridge: Cambridge University Press, 1938.

Curl, James Stevens, *European Cities and Society.* London: Leonard Hill, 1970.

Daunton, Martin, *House and Home in the Victorian City.* London: Edward Arnold, 1983.

Davidoff, L., *The Best Circles.* London: Croom Helm, 1973.

Delort, Robert, *Life in the Middle Ages.* Transl. by Robert Allen. London: Phaidon, 1974.

De Vries, J., *European Urbanization 1500-1800.* Cambridge, Massachusetts: Harvard University Press, 1984.

Dickinson, Robert, *City and Region.* London: Routledge & Kegan Paul, 1964.

Dollinger, Philippe, *The German Hansa.* Transl. and ed. by D. S. Ault and S. H. Steinberg. Stanford: Stanford University Press, 1970.

Dunn, Ross E., *The Adventures of Ibn Battuta.* London: Croom Helm, 1986.

Elliott, Brent, *Victorian Gardens.* London: Batsford, 1986.

Elvin, Mark, *The Pattern of the Chinese Past.* Stanford: Stanford University Press, 1973.

Evans, R. J., *Death in Hamburg.* Oxford: Clarendon Press, 1987.

Fanshawe, H. C., *Delhi, Past and Present.* London: John Murray, 1902.

Ferguson, John, and Kitty Chisholm, eds., *Political and Social Life in the Great Age of Athens.* London: Ward Lock, 1978.

Finley, Moses, *The Ancient Economy.* London: Hogarth, 1985.

Fossati, Gildo, *Monuments of Civilisation: China.* Milan: Mondadori, 1982.

Fossier, Robert, ed., *The Cambridge Illustrated History of the Middle Ages.* Vol. 3, 1250-1520. Transl. by Sarah Hanbury Tenison. Cambridge: Cambridge University Press, 1986.

Frankfort, Henri, *The Pelican History of Art: The Art and Architecture of the Ancient Orient.* Harmondsworth, England: Penguin Books, 1970.

George, M. Dorothy, *London Life in the XVIIIth Century.* London: Kegan Paul, Trench, Trubner, 1930.

Gernet, Jacques, *Daily Life in China on the Eve of the Mongol Invasion 1250-1276.* Transl. by H. M. Wright. London: Allen & Unwin, 1962.

Gies, Joseph, and Frances Gies, *Life in a Medieval City.* New York: Crowell, 1969.

Girouard, Mark, *Cities & People.* New Haven: Yale University Press, 1985.

Glaab, C., and A. T. Brown, *A History of Urban America.* New York: Macmillan, 1976.

Green, Peter, *A Concise History of Ancient Greece to the Close of the Classical Era.* London: Thames and Hudson, 1973.

Grimal, P., *Roman Cities.* Ed. and transl. by G. M. Woloch. Madison: University of Wisconsin Press, 1983.

Gutkind, E. A., *Urban Development in Western Europe.* Vols. 4 and 5. New York: The Free Press, 1971.

Haeger, John Winthrop, ed., *Crisis and Prosperity in Sung China.* Tucson: University of Arizona Press, 1975.

Hall, John W., and Jeffrey P. Mass, eds., *Medieval Japan.* New Haven: Yale University Press, 1974.

Hall, Peter, *Cities of Tomorrow.* Oxford: Basil Blackwell, 1988.

Hay, Denys, ed., *The Age of the Renaissance.* New York: McGraw, 1967.

Hayes, John R., ed., *The Genius of Arab Civilisation.* Oxford: Phaidon, 1978.

Herlihy, David, *Medieval and Renaissance Pistoia.* New Haven: Yale University Press, 1967.

Heyden, Doris, and Paul Gendrop, *Pre-Columbian Architecture of Mesoamerica.* Transl. by Judith Stanton. London: Faber and Faber, 1988.

Hibbert, Christopher:
Cities and Civilizations. London: Weidenfeld and Nicolson, 1987.
London: The Biography of a City. London: Longmans, 1969.
Rome: Biography of a City. Harmondsworth, England: Penguin Books, 1985.

Hitti, Philip K., *Capital Cities of Arab Islam.* Minneapolis: University of Minnesota Press, 1973.

Hodges, Richard, and David Whitehouse, *Mohammed, Charlemagne and the Origins of Europe.* London: Duckworth, 1983.

Hohenberg, P. M., and L. Lees, *The Making of Urban Europe, 1000-1950.* Cambridge, Massachusetts: Harvard University Press, 1985.

Hourani, A. H., and S. M. Stern, eds., *The Islamic City.* Oxford: Bruno Cassirer and University of Pennsylvania Press, 1970.

Ibn Battuta, *The Travels of Ibn Battuta.* Ed. and transl. by Hamilton Gibb. Cambridge: Hakluyt Society, 1971.

Ibn Jubayr, *The Travels of Ibn Jubayr.* Transl. by R. J. C. Broadhurst. London: Jonathan Cape, 1967.

Jellicoe, Sir Geoffrey, et al., eds., *The Oxford Companion to Gardens.* Oxford: Oxford University Press, 1986.

Jones, Emrys, and Eleanor Van Zandt, *The City.* London: Aldus Books / Jupiter Books, 1974.

Joyce, Patrick, *Work, Society and Politics.* New Brunswick: Rutgers University Press, 1980.

Juvenal, *Satires.* Ed. by Peter Green. Harmondsworth, England: Penguin, 1967.

Koenigsberger, H. G., *Medieval Europe 400-1500.* Harlow, England: Longman, 1987.

Kostof, Spiro, *America by Design.* Oxford: Oxford University Press, 1987.

Kramer, S. N., *The Sumerians.* Chicago: University of Chicago Press, 1963.

Krautheimer, Richard, *Rome. The Profile of a City.* Princeton: Princeton University Press, 1980.

Lane, Frederick C., *Venice: A Maritime Republic.* Baltimore: The Johns Hopkins University Press, 1973.

Lapidus, Ira Marvin, *Muslim Cities in the Later Middle Ages.* Cambridge, Massachusetts: Harvard University Press, 1967.

Lassner, Jacob, *The Topography of Baghdad in the Early Middle Ages.* Detroit: Wayne State University Press, 1970.

Lewis, Bernard, ed., *The World of Islam.* London: Thames and Hudson, 1976.

Lloyd, Seton:
The Archaeology of Mesopotamia. London: Thames and Hudson, 1978.
The Art of the Ancient Near East. London: Thames and Hudson, 1961.

Louis-Frederic, *Daily Life in Japan at the Time of the Samurai, 1185-1603.* Transl. by E. M. Howe. New York: Praeger, 1972.

Macaulay, Rose, *The Pleasure of Ruins.* London: Weidenfeld and Nicolson, 1953.

McCall, Andrew, *The Medieval Underworld.* London: Hamish Hamilton, 1979.

McKay, J. P., *Tramways and Trolleys.* Princeton: Princeton University Press, 1976.

McMullan, John L., *The Canting Crew.* New Brunswick: Rutgers University Press, 1984.

Marshall, Sir John, ed., *Mohenjo-daro and the Indus Civilization.* London: Arthur Probsthain, 1931.

Mehling, F., ed., *Phaidon Cultural Guide to Greece.* Oxford: Phaidon, 1985.

Michell, George, ed., *Architecture of the Islamic World.* London: Thames and Hudson, 1978.

Morris, Ian, *Burial and Ancient Society.* Cambridge: Cambridge University Press, 1987.

Morton, H. V., *The Waters of Rome.* London: The Connoisseur and Michael Joseph, 1966.

Mumford, Lewis, *The City in History.* London: Secker & Warburg, 1961.

Mundy, John H., and Peter Riesenberg, *The Medieval Town.* Princeton: D. Van Nostrand, 1958.

Murray, Oswyn, *Early Greece.* London: Fontana, 1980.

Nissen, H. J., *The Early History of the Ancient Near East, 9000-2000 B.C.* Chicago: University of Chicago Press, 1988.

Norwich, John Julius, ed., *The Italian World.* London: Thames and Hudson, 1983.

Olsen, D., *The City as a Work of Art.* New Haven: Yale University Press, 1986.

Oppenheim, A. Leo, *Ancient Mesopotamia.* Chicago: University of Chicago Press, 1977.

Parke, H. W., *Festivals of the Athenians.* London: Thames and Hudson, 1977.

Pennick, Nigel, *The Ancient Science of Geomancy.* London: Thames and Hudson, 1979.

Petry, Carl F., *The Civilian Elite of Cairo in the Later Middle Ages.* Princeton: Princeton University Press, 1981.

Pirenne, Henri, *Medieval Cities.* Transl. by F. D. Halsey. Princeton: Princeton University Press, 1952.

Platt, C., *The English Medieval Town.* London: Secker & Warburg, 1976.

Polo, Marco, *The Travels.* Ed. and transl. by Ronald Latham. London: Penguin, 1958.

Reps, J., *Making of Urban America.* Princeton: Princeton University Press, 1965.

Rich, J. W., and Andrew Wallace-Hadrill, eds., *City and Country in the Ancient World.* London: Routledge, 1990.

Roche, Daniel, *The People of Paris.* Transl. by Marie Evans. London: Berg, 1987.

Rörig, Fritz, *The Medieval Town.* London: Batsford, 1967.

Rosenau, Helen, *The Ideal City.* London: Studio Vista, 1974.

Rossbach, Sarah, *Feng Shui.* New York: Sutton, 1983.

Russell, Dorothea, *Medieval Cairo and the Monasteries of Wādi Natrūn.* London: Weidenfeld and Nicolson, 1962.

Rykwert, Joseph, *The Idea of a Town.* Princeton: Princeton University Press, 1976.

Scarre, Chris, ed., *Past Worlds: The Times Atlas of Archaeology.* London: Times Books, 1988.

Shelston, Dorothy, and Alan Shelston, *The Industrial City 1820-1870.* London: Macmillan, 1990.

Sjoberg, Gideon, *The Preindustrial City, Past and Present.* Glencoe: The Free Press, 1960.

Snodgrass, Anthony, *Archaic Greece.* London: J. M. Dent, 1980.

Staffa, Susan Jane, *Conquest and Fusion: The Social Evolution of Cairo: A.D. 642-1850.* Leiden: E. J. Brill, 1977.

Stambaugh, John E., *The Ancient Roman City.* Baltimore: The Johns Hopkins University Press, 1988.

Stow, John, *A Survey of London.* Oxford: Clarendon Press, 1908.

Sutcliffe, Anthony, ed., *Metropolis 1890-1940.* London: Mansell, 1984.

Tacitus, *Agricola.* Transl. by M. Hutton, revised by R. M. Ogilvie. Cambridge, Massachusetts: Harvard University Press, 1970.

Timms, Edward, and David Kelley, eds., *Unreal City.* New York: St. Martin's Press, 1985.

Toynbee, Arnold, ed., *Cities of Destiny.* New York: McGraw, 1967.

Trigger, B. G., et al., *Ancient Egypt. A Social History.* Cambridge: Cambridge University Press, 1983.

Tuchman, Barbara, *A Distant Mirror.* New York: Knopf, 1978.

Wacher, J. S., *The Towns of Roman Britain.* Berkeley: University of California Press, 1975.

Walbank, F. W., *The Hellenistic World.* London: Fontana, 1981.

Ward-Perkins, J. B., *Cities of Ancient Greece and Italy.* London: Sidgwick & Jackson, 1974.

Warner, S. B., *The Urban Wilderness.* New York: Harper & Row, 1972.

Weber, Max, *The City.* Transl. and ed. by Don Martindale and Gertrude Neuwirth. New York: The Free Press, 1958.

Webster, T. B. L., *Everyday Life in Classical Athens.* London: Batsford, 1969.

Wheeler, Sir Mortimer, *Civilizations of the Indus Valley and Beyond.* London: Thames and Hudson, 1966.

Wiet, Gaston, *Cairo, City of Art and Commerce.* Transl. by Seymour Feiler. Norman: University of Oklahoma Press, 1964.

Williams, Gwyn, *Medieval London.* London: Athlone Press, 1963.

Winslow, E. M., *A Libation to the Gods.* London: Hodder and Stoughton, 1963.

Wohl, A. S., *Endangered Lives: Public Health in Victorian Britain.* London: Dent, 1983.

Woolley, Sir Leonard, *Ur of the Chaldees.* London: Herbert Press, 1982.

Wrigley, E. A.:
City and Region: A Geographical Interpretation. London: Routledge & Kegan Paul, 1972.
Continuity, Chance and Change. Cambridge: Cambridge University Press, 1988.

Wycherley, R. E., *How the Greeks Built Cities.* New York: Norton, 1962.

Ziegler, Philip, *The Black Death.* London: Collins, 1969.

PICTURE CREDITS

INDEX